Go Ahead,

Rock the Boat!

Michael HH Warren

Cover design by Robin D. Bruce Smith and Konrad Schaffner
Edited by Theresa Lütge-Smith

ISBN-13: 978-1535232937
ISBN-10: 1535232935

Printed in the United States of America

Contents

Dedication v

Author's Note vii

Preface 1

Introduction 3

Chapter I Kibbutz 5

Chapter II Flying Start 33

Chapter III Road of Trials 53

Chapter IV Heroes' Journey 83

Chapter V Spiritual Counterculture 109

Chapter VI Value of Significance 127

Author's Closing Note 151

Acknowledgments 153

Dedication

I dedicate this book to Kelly & Caden and Generation Z.

The times are changing, the world is changing and Generation Z holds the key to a future that understands modern technology, entrepreneurship and diversity better than anyone.

The challenges to be faced will be equal if not greater than those of their forefathers, but armed with the tools of a modern world, there is a renewed, even brighter future ahead.

The biggest lesson in life remains—if you fail, get up, dust yourself off and try again.

You are our future and will be taking this world into unknown and unchartered territories—be prepared!

This work is a tribute to you.

Michael HH Warren
July 2016

Author's Note

Because life affords us with choices, we can either steer our boat into calm waters, paralyzed by fear and complacency, or we can purposely make waves, by taking risks, daring to be different, challenging convention, so that we may raise the sails and soar in the breeze!

It is my sincere hope and wish that schools and colleges will make this book part of their reading studies.

Michael HH Warren
July 2016

Preface

YOUNG PEOPLE TODAY are at a crossroads. Older generations fail to connect with them on most levels, arguing they are ungrateful, narcissistic and entitled.

"Whatever they have at their disposal is never good enough; they're opinionated; once you succumb to a demand it becomes an expectation; they shun the reality that if you want something you must work to afford it; not only are they labeled as lazy, uninspired and non-committal, their inflated sense of entitlement about earnings, leisure, and career progression confirm their adverse impression of what an emerging young adult traditionally personifies. They are a matchless peer group branded Generation Z." NOT A FLATTERING PORTRAYAL, nor apparently does it bode well for the future leadership of the human race.

On the plus side, while they might be less politically engaged than expected, they are environmentally and socially conscious, less materialistic, more community-minded and less cynical compared to previous generations.

Generation Z wants to change the world; fame and fortune isn't top-most on their agenda but having a positive impact on the world is.

They usually operate in small, tight-knit groups, comprise nearly two billion people globally, and are intent on creating a new and better future. In short, their response is valid.

"No one recognizes that our branded conduct is a depiction of our anger at the world we live in; angry that we will have to restore the planet

despite older generations holding us in contempt, analyzing our responses as though we are a nonentity. We believe that social justice is the truest way of accomplishing this.

Like Plato's allegory of the cave, the exchange of viewpoints among peers is an attempt to explain the nature of reality and clarify the source of absolute knowledge! The intention of quick-witted repartee and thoughtful problem-solving is to stimulate critical thinking to illuminate ideas about universal questions on erosion of national pride and identity, politics, religion, poverty, education disparity, materialism, substance abuse, and single parent households, amongst others."

As spiritualism and mysticism weave their spells, most teens and young adults today have an absorbing interest in the unknown, the unseen and the future. Yet, for many their hopes, ambitions, and plans are permeated with the subconscious fear that perhaps there will be no future at all for mankind.

The reasons for their psychosis are fascinating and extremely relevant to this hour of history in which we live. The world is in a mess—pollution, congestion, urban sprawl, widespread famine, increased illiteracy, civil unrest and unemployment threaten the foundations of public order. These are only some of the concerns.

Those on the outside proclaim loudly the responsibility they face, asking "Where are we going? How can we protect ourselves? How can we help others?"

Introduction

Five teenage friends find themselves at odds with their families, culture and social standing. They find solace within their group. Their choices are shaped by changes within the global economy and exposure to cultural diversity, rapid technological development, and the difficulty of cultivating dependable relationships.

The friends nurture the hopes, ideals, and positive qualities in each other, ideals that grow in response to the state of the world economy, the spread of technologies, and generally the turbulent times in which we live.

Together they travel to Israel to embark on a one-month working holiday at the Beit Nir Kibbutz, located between the cities of Beit Shemesh and Kiryat Gat. Here they find a meaningful and consistent home with socially and environmentally responsible values.

They yearn for work that allows the worker to feel like they are contributing to something bigger than themselves. They socialize with the locals, learning some Hebrew and Arabic, and the history of the Middle East.

They immerse themselves in Israeli life and culture, work alongside and engage in dialogues with Jewish Israelis, Israeli-Arabs and Bedouins who are striving for a just and lasting peace. The friends engage in subsistence apprenticeships, from working in the fruit orchards to running the chicken coops.

The group tests their friendship and evolved sentiments relevant to global social ills affecting mankind and their generation through conversations, by exploring diverse viewpoints, including the impact of the Israeli-Palestinian Conflict and its similarity to, and divergence from, South Africa's former Apartheid regime.

Their search is for new ways to learn from today to better prepare for the future, to increase tolerance and decrease materialism, parallel to evoking justifiable critical thinking about authority and government.

But there is much more at play here than just creating boundaries between old and new philosophies: in deciphering the enmeshed friendship bond within the troupe, the intention is to engender a metamorphic and ground-breaking leap of mindsets.

Chapter I

Kibbutz

The airport lounge was abuzz with passengers and palpable with excitement. The five friends, attired in their designer-label garb strutted toward a ramshackle mini bus, displaying the name Beit Nir in bold lettering. They travelled for a couple of hours through scenic farmlands.

Not much was said during the trip, as the newness of their surroundings inspired a childlike exuberance.

"On the left you will see our large housing project, occupied mostly by Asian-African and American-European immigrants," the bus driver announced.

"This region is steeped in history; there are hundreds of ancient man-made chalk caves you may want to explore," he added.

"What were these caves used for?" Emma, her inquisitive nature getting the better of her, instinctively leaned forward as she spoke.

"Over the course of two thousand years people used them as quarries, stables and granaries."

"I read somewhere early civilizations also used the caves as water cisterns and workspaces for pressing grapes and olives," remarked Zach.

"And as cultic houses of worship, I believe," he added as the bus driver nodded in agreement.

"Is Beit Nir essentially an agri-business?" asked Connor.

'Most certainly! The Kibbutz grows wheat, oranges and cotton, and produces olive oil. We also operate a cattle ranch and chicken houses," the bus driver said proudly. *He loved sharing his knowledge with newcomers to the area.*

Zach, Emma, Jon, Lea, and Connor had become close friends after meeting at an Inter-denominational Youth Camp for teens, held at a farm in South Africa's KwaZulu-Natal province. This event took place when they were in Grade 7. They had kept in touch through social networking and had been planning this working holiday for the past three years. Shared information centered mostly on the latest music downloads, sharing photos on Instagram, micro-blogging and posting jokes on Twitter. The friends, just having written their grade 10 examinations, have important decisions to make regarding their tertiary education. Each of the friends had recently celebrated their sixteenth birthday. This was their December vacation before embarking on the final two years of mainstream schooling. They were excited: it was good to be back together.

***

Social ills today include a steady erosion of national pride and identity, politics and religion, as well as growing global poverty, educational disparity, materialism, substance abuse, and prevalence of single parent households, amongst others.

Young people today are not sheltered from the atrocities that threaten human survival. They know that absolutely nothing that happens on Earth is an accident. Every war, environmental devastation or man-made disaster, and pandemic is part of a grand scheme to manipulate and control mankind.

Genetic engineering is only one example how nature is redesigned and rebuilt. The term *playing God* is linked to this *science*; even insects are being weaponized for combat, and the fear that humans are by no means exempt from being transformed is making them question their own mortality.

It might sound farfetched, but Generation Z; today's teens and emerging adults, pride themselves on being morally conscious. In defining the religious beliefs of today's typical teen it is understood that their overt version of religious faith is one where God is remote from His creation.

They support the idea that they need to be virtuous and live moral lives, but find the definition of *morality* ambiguous.

Similarly, high numbers of teens question the definition of *absolute truth*; most simply believe it is up to individuals to determine what defines *being truthful and honest*. They're comfortable holding conflicting ideas in tension with one another, relevant to their friends' individualistic opinions, religious, political and cultural beliefs. Their notion of separating Jesus Christ from the Church or being spiritual without being religious, stems from a lack of meaningful relationships. It is difficult to call teens to a relationship with Christ when they don't know what a relationship is.

Generation Z want a meaningful life that's going to have a positive impact on future generations. Their struggle is driven by *a hunger for truth and absolute knowledge.*

They want something more real than what modern society is currently giving them, yet many are undecided whether there is any standard of right and wrong.

Truth is different for each individual; it has its own reality, its own logic, and its own interpretation of right and wrong.

***

The new arrivals were escorted to a two-storey house set in a lush garden, an oasis where it never rains. The forest within the compound contained natural springs, carpets of wild flowers, olive orchards and agricultural plots on ancient agricultural terraces.

The cobbled-stone path leading to the front door looked ancient, as if it had been there for centuries, Zach remarked as they entered it. The modest house had an aura of history, with stonework reminiscent of early 18th Century architecture.

Beyond the door the new tenants entered a central courtyard with a number of rooms opening off it. The bedrooms were small and dark with a minimum of windows; latticework and shutters covered the window openings. Each bedroom had a single bed, desk and chair, and a cupboard with fresh linens and towels.

"This will be your home for the next four weeks," a stout women in her fifties gestured. "There is one communal dormitory with three beds, two separate single rooms, lounge, kitchen, toilet and shower. Breakfast and lunch is provided in the cafeteria; dinner is your own responsibility," she added, handing Zach the key.

A wooden staircase led up onto the roof, which was used as an outdoor patio, partly shaded by matting. The indoor courtyard doubled as a lounge; the room was furnished with several couches, lounge chairs and a television.

The Kosher kitchen was equipped with two distinct preparation and cooking areas, and an odd array of crockery, cooking utensils and cutlery. They unpacked their things and headed for the dining hall about 100 meters away along a path.

"I'm starving!" said Zach.

"Wonder what's on the menu; hope it's nice!" commented Lea.

"Don't get your hopes up, I hear Kibbutz food sucks!" Jon chipped in.

"Even so, no dinner? Are we to resort to hunter-gatherer survival mode?" Emma said jokingly.

"Fortunately I brought along some pumpkin seeds; we can grow our own food!" said Jon.

"Or we can forage the garden for wild herbs and mushrooms," said Lea pragmatically.

"Very funny," said Zach. He was really hungry. The prospect of foraging for herbs and mushrooms did not amuse him.

The dining hall was the size of a small airplane hangar, with dark wooden floors. The floor space was occupied with rows of steel tables and chairs. The place was spotless.

A long queue had formed at the far wall where kitchen staff

handed each person food dished up in a tin plate. The moment the group entered the dining hall, all eyes were on them.

"What's up … do we look odd or what?" whispered Zach.

The friends soon learned that residents wore a uniform of regular blue denim jeans and a plain white tee shirt. The reason for the odd stares was because they stood out like sore thumbs, sporting black skinny jeans ripped at the knees; tee shirts imprinted with outrageous graphics of skulls and Hollywood icons, and cropped leather biker jackets. The boy's had partially shaved heads while the girls flaunted Harajuku hairstyles in crimson and various other colors. They definitely looked out of place.

The dining hall was the place where everything happened; the food was just a tiny and almost insignificant part of what went on there.

Their first meal in Israel began with challah, which they broke at sunset. This was followed by a traditional meal of honey breaded chicken, which was delicious. There was also a choice of salads on a side table for residents to help themselves: tomato, beetroot and cucumber harvested from the kitchen garden. There were no negative comments about the cuisine. They cleaned their plates of every morsel before traipsing back to the house.

En route they met with two locals, Daniel and Rachel, who were in charge of allocating jobs to the new recruits. As a means to smooth the progress of group integration, the new workers were paired up with volunteers from other countries.

Zach was designated the role of working in the chicken coops; Lea would work in the laundry, Emma in the kitchen, Connor in the juice factory, and Jon in the fields.

They were told an allowance of 400 Shekels would be paid in advance as remuneration for their labor over the next four weeks, which was met with a jubilant applause for the monetary incentive.

"Take a stroll around the Kibbutz to familiarize yourselves with the surroundings and your new home," Daniel suggested.

The Kibbutz was a typical farm with cows, chickens, crops and a fruit orchard. There was a small shop where basic necessities like toiletries, milk, juice, and groceries were sold.

"You can run a tab if you like, and pay it at month end," Daniel advised.

Unfortunately at the time the friends did not realize that the monthly allowance was in fact a subsistence grant for them to buy their own dinner. The only alternative plan to get something to eat after a day's work was to hitchhike to the nearest town, which was 15 kilometers away.

Back at their residence, the friends explored the place. It seemed weird that this relic from the past was wired for electricity, but it prompted Emma to check the pantry and fridge for groceries.

The supplies were sparse: there was a tin of instant coffee, sugar, tea, milk, bread and butter. "Coffee anyone?" she asked, reaching for the mugs hanging from cup hooks on the wall-mounted shelf. She was greeted by a unanimous and resounding, "*Yes*, please!"

Emma carried a tray of coffee mugs to the lounge in the courtyard.

The perfume emitted by the Jasmine creeper covering the archway leading to the rooms was intoxicating. The courtyard contained a variety of culinary herbs growing in large terracotta pots, hand-woven floor rugs and several well-stocked bookshelves.

The weary travelers welcomed the opportunity to relax. The two girls sat on the edge of a small rock pond, swirling their hands in the cool water. It provided a soothing contrast to the parched landscape beyond the courtyard's walls.

"What have you guys been doing since Church Camp?" asked Jon, addressing the group.

Zach was first to respond.

"Living in Texas is pretty great. Ya'll have to visit; we'd have the greatest time ropin' and ridin' wild animals at the rodeo in Wichita Falls. Other than Whitetail deer hunting in Hill Country with my father and uncles, I wasted my time doing a course in Hospitality, on the insistence of my parents. Eighteen months of doing mundane chores, cleaning toilets, serving pompous guests, smiling idiotically at their feeble jokes. I gave up every weekend and school vacation. But this working-holiday is going to be a ball!" Zach could hardly contain his enthusiasm.

"Man, you are spoilt! I would give anything to learn new skills, there's always a chance of getting a job in the hospitality industry. Instead I looked after my sick mother for two years until her death last year; she had inoperable cancer. The cold British weather kept her indoors much of the time but each year she would spend time observing the Bewick's swans that migrate from Arctic Russia to Slimbridge, near our home. It was bitterly cold, but we wrapped up warmly. It was wonderful to see her joy for life. It was a magnificent sight; over 300 of these graceful Siberian swans occupied the vast wetlands reserve. There's nothing worse than watching someone you love die a slow painful death. I will forever remember that day. It had such a spiritual connotation for both of us because the arrival of this flock was the earliest in recorded history. According to experts this was a sign of a long, hard winter ahead. Mom died a week later," Emma cried.

"I'm sad for your loss Emma, you are a wonderful person having devoted your time to care for your Mom, but Zach has a point, life is too short to waste it on something you do not find inspiring! The land down under is still the best place to call home; there's nowhere in the world quite like Australia. I've done nothing spectacular these past four years, just went to school and stayed at home feeling depressed, until I picked up a book by Dr. Paul Brunton, *"A Hermit in the Himalayas"*. It changed my perspective on life, a profound spiritual experience! I had been stressing about getting into debt to pay off a study loan, but thankfully I qualify for a government youth allowance for when I start university. My parents are not wealthy enough to pay the fees," Lea explained.

"It seems each of our lives thus far have been influenced by some or other significant impact. My circumstances changed radically when my older sister moved to Tokyo to start a career in Marine Biology. We know her plane landed at Haneda Airport, but she vanished. She's been missing for almost three years; it has devastated our family! Things got so bad at home that my grades plummeted. My folks decided it would be better if I lived in school residence. So, I'm a boarder at my school in Christchurch, which is great. I've even taken up cycling. Our school team cycled from the alpine Aoraki Mt Cook village to the historic harbor town of Oamaru. The trail took us along the shores of the South Pacific Ocean, which has become New Zealand's number one cycle trail," Connor exclaimed.

Jon got to his feet abruptly. His face looked stricken. "This is whack; we've volunteered to experience life at a Kibbutz, to grow as human beings, to help those less fortunate, to come up with fresh ideas; this adventurous journey will inwardly prepare us for the demands and struggles of modern life. Sorry to hear about all your gripes and hassles, but glad you guys also made some great memories. What do you say we find out what this place is all about! Are you with me?"

Jon's intervention had the desired effect; the mood changed from somber to assertive.

"Hang on, you haven't told us what's been on your agenda these past three years," Zach interjected.

Jon looked uncomfortable, as if he wanted to run away. His pronounced exhale was an indication that a story to top all stories was about to be told.

"As you all know, my father owned a successful banana plantation in the Nkwaleni Valley in Zululand, but the family lost everything due to a bad business decision. We had to sell our house, furniture and everything we had, including the farm. My parents and six children, me included, were destitute.

We moved to a small house in Inanda, a fringe settlement near Durban in South Africa's KwaZulu-Natal province. Money was scarce. We all slept on the floor in one room. We were always hungry. Residents treated us kids like we didn't belong, as if we were scroungers. We blamed our father for the terrible poverty we had to endure.

A year later my second-eldest brother caught an infectious disease; we took him to the clinic but no matter what the doctors tried, his condition did not improve. My very talented 18-year old brother, who was destined to become a great athlete, died."

The group sat in stunned abeyance listening to Jon's story. Thinking he had concluded his tale, they reached for their coffee, as Jon continued.

"That following summer the eldest son, my 24-year old brother, caught a cold which eventually turned nasty. He grew weaker and weaker. Despite all our desperate efforts, my parents' eldest child, simply would not recover. He became the second family casualty within less than a year. I am still haunted by my mother's anguished face and drooping shoulders, but despite all the hardships my parents dote on me and put all their hopes on their only remaining son."

"You will never disappoint your family. You are a very good and kind person," said Emma tenderly.

The room became silent again. Everyone was thinking about what Jon had just told them. A copy of *The Jerusalem Post* newspaper on the couch caught Zach's attention. The headline "Israel preparing for possible influx of Syrian refugees" made him wonder whether Europe's refugee crisis was perhaps a result of the onslaught of militant Islam in the Middle East and in Africa that is causing people to flee from the worst crimes and violence that humanity has seen since World War II.

"What's your take on the erosion of national pride and identity?" Zach asked the group.

"Education is the key!" said Connor.

"Wish in one hand and spit in the other!" added Lea.

"Education is important; knowledge provides people with an increased chance of taking advantage of opportunities to be successful in life, to prepare them to compete in a job market with their peers!" said Emma.

"National pride should be a point of motivation that enables even ordinary citizens to seek solutions for their country's shortcomings and social ills," contributed Jon.

"Wow, the loss of national pride is probably our generation's biggest problem. I believe the main culprits are unemployment, poverty, poor education, food shortage and fear of civil unrest!" said Zach.

"What about corruption?"

"Absolutely! The most serious problem today is that the heads of countries lack integrity and honesty ... they fail at finding solutions to grow their national economy and education due to greed and lack of leadership in elected officials. Politicians are more concerned with being re-elected and manipulating their taxpayers to continue feeding at the trough than they are with solving the problems that plague their citizens. Social ills set in motion an increased flow of refugees and asylum seekers," said Emma, thinking of her home country, whilst Jon nodded his head sagely.

"What's the route for worldwide de-population?" asked Zach.

"War!" exclaimed Connor, his mock sarcasm given away with a delayed wink towards Lea.

"Typical anarchist mindset!" said Lea, tongue in cheek.

"The massive exodus into Europe is testimony of this. The erosion of national pride and identity, and culture and religion is inevitable!" said Emma, speaking from first-hand experience.

"The majority of refugees are intent on choosing the country with the most attractive economy as opposed to seeking a safe haven separate from their own despotic regime!" remarked Jon.

"I agree; while it may be true that refugees are fleeing to escape a Holocaust situation, they are equally motivated by the lure of materialism and an economically stable lifestyle in another country. In terms of the erosion of national pride and identity, a much larger threat to young people is the older generations who idealize their own upbringing and want to put progress in reverse to revert to the good old days!" said Zach, thinking of his family's traditional mindset.

"Your argument implies we've reached a point where a nation's culture is nearly antithetical to this ideal. If a country has been declining politically, socially, and economically isn't it fair to suggest that the biggest issue facing our generation today is the predominance of ever delusional baby-boomers who hold the next generation in such contempt in the first place?" asked Jon.

"There simply are too many people on earth; the world population is out of control!" stated Zach as a matter of fact.

"Sadly the means and methods of depopulation employed today are cruel. Exploitive international development leads to massive starvation. Close on 40-million deaths occur annually due to poor nourishment; then there's fomentation of war, hatred and military procurements leading to millions of deaths worldwide. And the orchestrated spread of infectious diseases leading to global pandemic, plague and pestilence!" said Jon with compassion.

"Admittedly, the previous century has been, by far the bloodiest in human history, motivated by despotic regimes of Mao, Pol Pot, Stalin, Hitler, and others!" commented Lea.

"What about nuclear, chemical and biological agents, weapons and warfare, the poisoning and contamination of the planet's food and water supplies, even weather modification that can lead to triggering earthquakes, volcanic eruptions and tsunamis?

"And what about the spreading of the deadly AIDS virus, forcing sterilization in countries such as China; even abortion?" Connor continued.

"Vastly unreported is the genocide occurring in the Congo where more than 4 million people have been slaughtered, mutilated and massacred recently with only scant world attention given!" Jon interjected.

"Add to this the unrestrained and very profitable build-up of weapons of mass destruction, nuclear, chemical and biological in the world!' he continued.

"Particularly in the Middle East region!" said Connor.

"And don't forget all of this is hurtling towards an Apocalypse of World War 3. The death toll of this war is predicted to surpass all previous in scale and in magnitude!" said Zach.

"Wow, it's no wonder so many people are on drugs; the prospect of being eliminated by some privileged ruling elite is stupefying. Imagine a population of zombie-like people roaming the earth, unaware of their fate!" commented Connor.

"Why do you think people ignore the dangers of drug and alcohol abuse?" Lea prompted.

"There was a time where virtually every actor was portrayed on screen with a cigarette or alcoholic beverage in hand. Smoking and drinking was implied as cool, as a result everyone was doing it, including kids," said Zach.

"I've seen kids as young as nine smoking a hookah pipe at

parties with their parents present."

"They think it's safe because the smoke is filtered through water!" added Lea.

"Parents are stupid; this is a case where ignorance is not bliss. Smoking a hookah exposes one to toxic chemicals and risk of infectious disease when hookahs are shared. It's the start to drug addiction and has the potential to cause lung cancer, respiratory illness, low birth weight in babies and periodontal disease!" said Zach.

"Many kids find it funny to boast about regularly getting wasted," said Connor.

"The sad reality is that parents can only do so much; dumb kids are going to do dumb things regardless of what era we live in. We can't blame the modern world for parents' inability to raise their children to be moral. Don't think everyone from 1940-1985 had a golden childhood filled with rainbows and sunshine!" said Emma.

"They may not have had perfect childhoods, but two decades ago parents at least instilled manners in their demon offspring. Now all parents do is give their kids everything they want so they'll shut up!" said Connor.

"Some parents just aren't bothered; they just want to get the kids out of their hair!" added Zach.

"People should have a license and undergo in-depth training before they're allowed to have children. Do they seriously expect children to raise themselves?" said Lea, suddenly grateful for the sacrifices her parents had made on her behalf.

"Parents need to take responsibility to raise their kids!" said Jon.

"I agree, even Aristotle complained about the youth 2300-odd years ago. He said, they have bad manners, contempt for authority, they show disrespect to their elders, they no longer rise when elders enter the room, they contradict their parents, chatter before company, gobble up dainties at the table, cross their legs, and are tyrants over their teachers," said Emma.

"The situation is even worse today. Many kids grow up in single-parent families, usually headed by a mother or grandmother. They deal with so many pressures!" Emma continued.

"Surely growing up in a single-parent household isn't all bad?" Connor intervened.

"My mother taught me the value of not only money, but the value of hard work, of being a truly good person, and for standing up for what's right. Even more importantly, no matter how many jobs my mother had, or how many courses she was taking through distance learning, she was there for me, always, when I woke up in the morning, when I went to bed at night, and whenever I needed a shoulder to cry on, ear to bend, or a little tough love. She was there, she still is!" said Connor.

"My mother is my best friend … she is one of the strongest and bravest people I know. I admire her; she is my hero. If I can be even half the mother that she is to me when I decide to start a family, I will be thrilled!" said Lea.

"I commend your respective mothers for doing such a great job raising you but you must admit doing such a commendable job is probably the exception rather than the rule. The facts of the matter are that children raised in single parent homes find themselves at a disadvantage when compared to children raised in two parent homes!" Zach countered.

"I agree—there's no denying that a generalization can be made. Two incomes, after all, are better than one, but I know few two parent families who have done a better job raising their children together than my mother did entirely alone!" said Jon after a few moments silence.

"I'm going to disagree with the assumption that two incomes are better than one. Look at it from another perspective... perhaps dual parent households are the problem!" Zach jumped in.

"Do you mean that dual incomes tend to inflate lifestyles, that children raised in this manner have a false sense of financial pragmatism?" Jon asked.

"I'm saying that one parent raising one child or possibly two children is completely realistic, and in my opinion ideal. It's insane to create false expectations but at the same time it's important to nurture a determined attitude!" said Zach, defending his point of view.

"Let's be realistic about this, the issues facing Japanese children or Russian children or African children are going to be entirely different than those found in Europe and the United States!" stated Connor.

"We cannot paint everyone with the same brush, nothing is ever that simplistic!" Emma reiterated.

"Developmental problems begin at home. The number of single parent homes has increased to the point of catastrophe. Today over 14 million single parents are responsible for rearing 28 million children!" said Zach.

"It's tough economically for most. What about the working poor, people who play by the rules but remain below the poverty line? In many cases kids are left alone during the day while the parent is away at work, increasing the risk that they will busy themselves with activities that are dangerous and subjected to a higher chance of drug and alcohol abuse!" said Lea with empathy.

"It truly takes a village to raise a child!" said Jon, thinking of his parents back home.

"Once I discovered a homeless family who had taken shelter in our garden shed. My family let them stay during the winter after which they moved on. Where they went to, I have no idea!" he added.

"It's interesting that two completely different classes interact in the same suburb, street, or sometimes even share the same address, but generally the rich ignore the poor while the poor harass the rich, begging for money, food and clothing!" said Lea.

"It is sad that the poor are forced to rummage for food and saleable items in refuse bags," said Jon.

"The rich have a tendency to frown upon the less fortunate

as if it was an irritation. There are not enough people who are prepared to help this terrible situation as it gets progressively worse!" remarked Lea.

"There is a great divide between the haves and the have not's. Of course it's not good to create a culture of dependency, endorsing a form of adverse entitlement where beggars do nothing to help improve their dilemma. In fact, beggars get angry when those with money are not charitable," Jon continued.

"My contention is to help where you can, but simply giving a beggar or homeless person some loose change isn't helping their situation. They pool their meager takings to buy drugs or alcohol, instead of food," he said.

"Do you blame them? Can you imagine how hard it must be to plead from passersby all day, only to be tossed some coins? Buying food is expensive! Besides, for every person parting with some loose change, many fob them off and walk on," Emma interjected.

"Yeah, it's a horrible existence for some. Have you ever been that hungry that you're willing to humiliate yourself begging someone to give you money, and risk being insulted and accused of being too lazy to find a job?" Zach asked.

"I know what it's like to be so hungry that your brain chemistry is negatively impacted; you can't concentrate or sleep," Jon added glumly.

"Consider that Western developed countries donate handout money to feed poor nations. In some instances welfare is a good thing, but people in charge of distributing the money to uplift communities are often corrupt. It is common knowledge that government officials steal the money to line their own pockets," said Emma with disdain.

"On the other hand, impoverished communities believe they are entitled to this free money. They blame their government for the lack of job opportunities," Jon contributed.

"For the most part welfare is beneficial if it helps society to function properly. The objective should be to give poor people an opportunity at life that they cannot provide for themselves, like skills training. Welfare should enable people to become more educated and get better jobs," Lea added.

"Shouldn't we give to others unconditionally if we have the means to do so?" Zach asked.

"Poverty is like a disease … it eats away at the fabric of society!" he added after the rest of the group nodded at one another.

"Do you think global poverty can ever be eradicated?" Jon prompted.

"The Industrial Revolution and the consequent rapid growth of world economies created a culture of dependency. Charity is all well and good, but it's naïve to think we can ever fully eradicate poverty," said Zach with confidence.

"They even quote Jesus as saying that we will always have the poor with us," he continued.

"Perhaps we should leave Jesus out of the poverty debate because it turns out this statement is anything but an excuse for apathy," Emma said assertively, taking a sip of her coffee.

"Yes, it's true. Jesus' quote alludes to the importance of helping those in need," Lea agreed.

"Surely there must be a universal solution to ending poverty?" Jon tried again.

"Because people who have nothing are robbed of their self-esteem, dignity and capacity to function as fully actualized human beings, many resort to criminal behavior in order to survive," Connor stated matter-of-factly.

"Mahatma Gandhi reiterates this sentiment, that poverty is the worst form of violence!" Jon said compassionately.

"Violent crime is escalating; there is no excuse for violence. Genocide is horrible, an abomination of humankind. It's totally unacceptable, no matter how destitute you are!" Connor finished.

"Prisons are over-crowded with murderers and criminals. Violent crime has escalated to the extent that people have turned crime into a legitimate career," said Zach thinking about his native country and its high rate of imprisonment.

"But what can the man on the street do to make a difference?" asked Connor.

"You mean 'person'," Lea chipped in.

"Every family needs a touch of poverty through old-fashioned frugality, and scale-back extravagant, often wasteful habits, to empathize with the plight of the poor!" Zach said.

"The key is to return to traditional values of harmony and balance with nature, and in building stronger personal interaction with other people, in particular those who are less fortunate!" Jon said.

"Living a simple life, although not one of deprivation, is a huge opportunity for society to stop being so materialistic!" Emma remarked.

"Not enough focus has been placed on what the poor can do to help themselves. They're more often cast as victims of misguided policies, and crippled by debt!" Jon said with feeling.

"The poor need access to knowledge on becoming financially literate. Many have never had a bank account. It's these knowledge gaps that perpetuate poverty!" added Zach.

"There's only one effective solution to world poverty. It is the only solution that has ever worked or will ever work. Poor nations must produce their own prosperity; the Industrial Revolution nations produced their own wealth; the same pattern has continued in the modern era!" said Emma with quite some passion.

"Japan grew from being a poor agricultural economy to the world's second-largest economy by manufacturing cars, electronics and ships. The same can be said for previously poor nations like South Korea, Chile and China. Every nation that has escaped poverty has done so by producing its own prosperity!" commented Connor.

"And, as mentioned earlier, foreign aid given through the governments of poor countries does more harm than good. It entrenches corrupt rulers, fattens their personal bank accounts, and fuels civil unrest over control of the nation's treasury!" said

Jon.

"Charitable aid from affluent nations by way of financial donations, food and medicine are important because they meet urgent needs but they are only addressing the symptoms of impoverished citizens namely starvation and disease, rather than the cause. This boils down to the fact that the recipient government is not producing its own prosperity!" added Lea.

"When Israel came into the Promised Land, God did not promise them constant donations of riches from other nations but hills filled with iron and copper and fields of vines and fig trees. God's blessing of prosperity would come as a result of productive work; even the poor had to work!" said Zach.

"Abundant natural resources are not always the answer for poor nations. Many African nations have immense resources yet they remain poor. Nations like Switzerland, Japan, Taiwan and Singapore all lack significant natural resources but have become wealthy by creating productive economies!" Jon added.

"What must a failing nation do to become more productive?" Connor asked.

"Citizens, the people whose vote put governments in charge, must address its government leaderships, its economic system, broad-based education, early childhood development, heightened productivity, and its cultural beliefs. National prosperity depends on a free market system, not a welfare state or socialism, or communism!" Jon answered him.

"A free market system is morally superior to every other economic system. It must include widespread access to private ownership of property, effective rule of law, a stable currency, increasing specialization in the workforce, free trade and lower taxes!" Lea added.

"But a free market system alone will not bring prosperity unless a nation also has the right kind of government and cultural beliefs!" Jon stated confidently. He was proud that despite their different nationalities and cultural contexts, his friends could hold mature, productive conversations with one another. Jon thought the world needed more of that.

"A government that focuses on nation building through the production of its own prosperity is one in which leaders are committed to safeguard important human freedoms, and set an example through moral leadership!" said Lea.

"There must also be good and wise cultural beliefs; to become truly productive a society must share a widespread belief in not stealing, being honest, working effectively and efficiently and using the earth's resources wisely." Connor added.

"In other words, living a moral life anchored in integrity and care for others!" Emma finished for him.

"Poverty is a complex problem ..."

***

It was dark outside by the time the teenagers finished their conversation. Emma produced a grass basket stocked with groceries: homemade bagels, goat cheese, fresh figs and a bottle of honey she had purchased from the supply store. She hurriedly placed seven plates on the table and distributed the food.

"An Epicurean delight, as my grandmother used to say," she said, excited to taste the goat's cheese that was made locally on the Kibbutz.

"There are two extra servings. Do we have guests joining us for dinner?" asked Lea.

"Yes, Daniel and Rachel will be here any minute now."

Daniel was in his mid-20s and married to Rachel. They had a 3-year old son Isaac. The couple had relocated from Tel Aviv when Isaac was born, to enjoy a simple rural lifestyle.

Earlier Daniel had told Emma that, from a financial point of view, building a home and family was much easier at the Beit Nir Kibbutz.

"There's also no stress, it's protective, everyone knows everyone, and there are strong community values," Daniel had explained.

The meal was scrumptious, the conversation enlightening. An appropriate end to a perfect day.

Zach entered the room with a tablecloth draped over his head and shoulders. He minced his way to an open area. His iPhone burst into full song. The *Hava Nagila* medley was his cue to demonstrate his version of the *Horah*, while lip-synching to the melodic voices portraying this famous Israeli folk song. His performance was a resounding crowd pleaser.

"*Encore, encore!*"

Tomorrow members of this assemblage would be scrubbing poop and traces of blood from newly-laid eggs;

frying those same eggs to serve breakfast to over one-hundred volunteers; sorting, washing and mending other people's dirty clothing and bedlinen; processing oranges for bottling and milking cows. Life was good.

So much to learn and pay forward.

Chapter II

Flying Start

The friends were wrapped in Sunday morning hibernation when a loud knock on the front door startled them to the reality that this was their first day to clock in for work. Within minutes they burst into the allotment, attired in blue jeans and white tee shirts, looking fresh-faced and eager.

"Grab some breakfast. The bus leaves in 15 minutes," Daniel said, smiling at their enthusiasm. He loved witnessing the metamorphoses that volunteers underwent at the Kibbutz. It was like everyone experienced an instant change of mood once they had settled down.

"Just for interest, Daniel, isn't it hectic to balance interfaith democracy with work schedules?" Connor asked him.

"About 20 percent of Israeli citizens are Muslim, Christian and Druze. We respect everyone's religious convictions," Daniel answered.

"What is Druze?" asked Lea with interest.

"The Israeli Druze is a distinct religious community of Arab descent. They live mainly in the north of the country," Daniel went on.

"The Kibbutz maintains strong connections with different denominations and various faiths; there is a growing need for dialogue between Jews, Christians and all religions," he finished.

"It is encouraging that people of this region are setting an example for the rest of the world that people can live meaningful and purposeful lives," said Emma chewing on a mouthful of fruit salad.

"Religious Faith is an individual's way of making sense of life and purpose," Daniel agreed with her.

Zach and Lea were the first to be dropped off. Emma had stayed on at the kitchen after their rushed breakfast. Connor and Jon journeyed into the countryside to join other volunteers assigned to picking oranges and milking cows.

It was a swelteringly hot day but they were unperturbed, excited to give of their best from day one. Job routines were explained and demonstrated in detail. It did not take long before strangers found commonalities that would sustain lifelong alliances across nationalities and bridge cultural diversity.

Many volunteers hated the work. They were peevish about having to shovel dirt, fearful of contamination, and the prospect of being reprimanded by a supervisor their own age if anyone slacked off.

Respite came in the form of a half hour lunchbreak. Those stationed near the cafeteria were more fortunate, having access to a sit-down meal of *Sambusak,* a semi-circular pocket of dough filled with beef, fried onions and spices.

The novice ranchers on the other hand were fed Potato Bourekas, a type of handmade bread, and oranges.

Lunch for Jon and Connor was followed by a quick game

of *Matkot*, a popular paddle ball game where players hit a small rubber ball with a wooden racket as many times as possible without dropping it.

"Come on, Zach; let's see how good you are at defense and offense!" one of the other volunteers shouted to the Texan as he finished his lunch.

"Wow, you really connect to this game!" After just a few moments of play Zach was impressed.

"It's fun and provides a great workout," his companion added.

"I know; there are no rules, there are no points, nothing. But it's a good sport," another volunteer chipped in on the conversation.

"It's a sport of Israel, like falafel," his companion said light-heartedly.

Jon focused his attention on the herd of cattle grazing in an enclosed paddock. He remembered how he had spent many hours on the farm with his father and brothers.

He was not feeling depressed but became acutely aware that being in this place, at this time was significant to his highest life purpose.

Until that moment he had not realized that he had kept a running account of what had happened to their family, tormenting himself through continuous self-talk, asking what it meant and how their broken family would endure the hardship of poverty.

His mind was constantly monitoring and interpreting, his

internal monologue fixed on negatively judging himself and others. Without hesitation he came to a sudden and profound understanding to take constructive action: *What can I learn from this? How can I improve? How can I help my family? How can I help humanity do better in evaluating life choices?*

Zach was always acting the fool; it was his way of avoiding confrontation. While his antics were entertaining to some, others were irritated by it. So when the Supervisor complained that the eggs were not properly washed, Zach proceeded to dance like a decapitated chicken.

He read the criticism on the faces of his audience instantly, and realized his clowning about was perhaps not a constructive comeback on his first day at work.

The process was simple: the eggs were to be retrieved from the chicken coop, washed and dried, and separated according to size before being packaged into carton containers. Not rocket science, but some ignoramuses kept getting the order of things wrong.

Despite the dull routine Zach was determined to do a good job and undertook to climb back into the chicken coop each day with vigor, packing eggs by the hundred.

He had Emma retrieve a plastic pot-scourer from the kitchen, which did a good job of cleaning the soiled eggs, to the delight of his supervisor.

Zach was also tasked with keeping nest boxes clean and replacing any dirty bedding.

On his own initiative he brushed down the walls, swept the

floor with a damp broom and collected the chicken poop and shavings to start a green compost heap. Zach, having regained his sense of decorum, laughingly announced that the smell of chicken poop would probably permeate his nostrils forever.

Everyone chuckled, nodding profusely. Despite his popularity, Zach had confidence in his abilities. "I'm not sure I can do this, but I think I can learn to with time and effort."

As a 16-year old Emma became panic-stricken as she stepped into the large Kibbutz kitchen. It was a hive of organized chaos. People in white jackets were power walking from station to stove to serving counter, loudly calling out unfamiliar jargon like *Coming Up On* and *Low-Board*.

It was all a bit intimidating. However for Emma this was a dream come true, having made up her mind to become a chef since she was about ten years old. She was elated at the prospect of being allowed to prep meals surrounded by stoves, steamers, workbenches, wall fridges and grills. She was full of anxiety about the future and was grateful for this opportunity.

A portly man in his50s handed her an oversized cook's jacket and a floppy white hat. It was then that she heard him give an instruction in Hebrew. Not understanding a word that was said added to her apprehension. Emma instinctively put on the jacket and hat believing this to be the obvious command.

The man burst out laughing, "I said please peel these potatoes." Emma quickly learned that Chef Shani was both loved and feared by his team, yet he was an inspiring leader.

Her job was to work at the prep station. Emma prepared

herself mentally for a 7 hour a day shift, six days a week. Emma thought of her mother, and how proud she would have been to see her daughter contributing to the kosher meals served at the Kibbutz.

At the end of her shift Chef Shani was so impressed that he offered Emma an unopened block of cheddar cheese and a Styrofoam container with delicious vegetables grown on the farm.

Lea had introduced herself to a group of women about the age of her mother. Their animated chatting continued uninterrupted as they bundled dirty laundry into large industrial washing machines, and sorted clean clothes and bedsheets. "So this is my job; seems simple enough!" she thought.

The manager assigned Lea to folding tee shirts and jeans, which challenged her dexterity to the extreme. Fortunately one of the women, much advanced in years than the other women working in the launderette, demoted Lea to folding towels.

"Thank you; my experience of doing my own laundry is non-existent I'm afraid. My mother always did it for me," Lea explained.

The old lady chuckled, "When I first came to the Kibbutz, I also didn't know anything about laundering."

The mountain of laundry was tackled with military precision.

"These women are masters of organization, and clearly physically in good shape," she thought.

Lea's muscles ached already. She had just meticulously

sorted items that needed ironing when a new challenge presented itself.

She fussed over trying to fold bottom sheets with elastic edges, but eventually got the hang of it. But frustration reduced her to tears when the neat pile of sheets toppled and fell to the floor. She was determined not to let this get her down, and picked up and re-folded each sheet.

Her next challenge was to master the sheet ironer, resulting in hours being enveloped in a fog of hot steam. Despite her discomfort, Lea noticed the other women nodding their approval. "Well done. You are learning," one said.

Lea thought of the book she had read; about the insight and discernment the writer had achieved from the holy men he had met on his journey in the Himalayas. The author had explained that we all needed 'oases of calm in a world of storm', no matter what era we were living in, and that to retreat from our everyday lives for a while was not weakness but strength.

Lea understood for the first time that by taking the trouble to discover the deep silence within, every person can find the benefits of being linked to an 'infinite power, an infinite wisdom, an infinite goodness'.

Folding and ironing laundry was not the kind of work she had envisaged she could accomplish, but she would not want it any other way.

The citrus plantation adjacent to the Kibbutz yielded three different varieties of oranges: the Shamouti orange, the navel orange and the bitter orange.

Connor loved the physical beauty of the landscape. The land looked prosperous and fertile, although in the midst of a sea of luscious green, were blotches of brown. They were plots of land where the citrus trees were no longer irrigated. The orange groves with their deep green leaves were broken up momentarily by dirt roads leading to a small fruit juice processing plant.

Connor joined a group of about ten volunteers as part of a *grove run* to hand-pick and deposit oranges into harvesting sacks that were manually dumped into 400 kg bins in the grove.

These bins were lifted by small trucks and taken to the edge of the grove where the oranges were deposited into a semi-trailer and transported to the factory. Connor felt the strain in his back, from reaching and picking the fruit continuously for five hours.

Following a short lunch break he walked to where he had noticed the patches of barren earth. He had saved four seeds from the orange he had been given as part of his lunch.

Impulsively he kneeled on the ground, dug four holes in the soil and surreptitiously planted the seeds. He watered the area from a plastic bottle, sharing his daily ration.

"This is in memory of you sis," he said.

On this day three years ago, his older sister had disappeared in Tokyo mysteriously. Connor remembered a poem she loved: *"When a flower is blooming it has reached its peak, and yet its glory is already set to fade. When it does so, it will form seeds for a new cycle to start."*

Each of the friends had encountered some form of adversity in their young lives, which is what brought them to this remote location in the first place.

Each had come face to face with inner-conflict, misfortune and sorrow.

They also failed to find a stable middle ground when expressing their views on prickly issues such as racial inequality, culling of endangered species for profit, and genocide.

They were stirred by an inner calling to delve into the unknown to gain clarity of as yet unmet challenges. *Where are we going? How can we protect ourselves? How can we help others?*

This had been the first day of their call to adventure. It had taken them into the unknown where their limitations navigated the unfamiliar until they crossed the abyss of death and rebirth through an altered mindset.

Each member of the group had undergone a subtle transformation through individual atonement before making their way back to reality.

Carl Jung once said, *"Until you make the unconscious conscious, it will direct your life and you will call it fate."*

The five childhood friends had a flying start to destroying a destructive mindset and emerging edified; they must use everything they have learned or Absolute Knowledge to get back to the ordinary world to help all who remain there.

It was almost 3 o'clock; it was time to head back to the Kibbutz. A trail of dust suggested that their ride was on schedule. Zach was the only passenger.

The bus filled up quickly as Connor, Jon and several of the other volunteers took their seats. Slowly the passengers began to bake in the intense, suffocating heat.

The bus trip was characterized by the pungent smell of unwashed bodies, yet every aching body was blissfully unaware of the stench

Emma and Lea were taken aback at the sight of the boys' filthy clothes and sunburnt faces, exchanging surprised looks in silence as the boys poured themselves cold drinks. They couldn't resist some humor.

"Did you guys spend the day in a pig pen?"

"Off to the shower with you!"

"Even your mothers wouldn't recognize you!"

***

It was Sunday evening, traditionally a laid-back time for many people. But here at the Beit Nir Kibbutz the entire community had gathered at the dining hall to enjoy good conversation, share gossip, feast on delicious food contributed by every household, and provide some comic relief.

The kind of entertainment that would have had most teenagers running for the hills now invited keen participation. The dining hall had been completely transformed. The tables were grouped at the back of the hall, where everyone placed their contributions of food for the communal feast. The chairs were organized in multiple rows to seat a good-sized audience. Facing the seating arrangement was a clearing, evidently intended to serve as a stage.

There was no formal program. The group of friends was excited to witness how this impromptu concert would play itself out. Party revelers took their seats and the lights were dimmed.

First on stage was Daniel; he was greeted by a resounding round of applause. The acoustics in the hall were surprisingly good.

Daniel's performance started off as a portrayal of a wannabe politician blurting out promises from a soapbox platform. His routine was familiar to the locals and seasoned volunteers, but still highly amusing.

Daniel went on to mimic being a drunken lout causing mischief in a bar; he staggered and fell while pretending to take a copious swig from a bottle. His moans and groans provoked members of the audience to shout out words of encouragement.

"Give us a song then!"

"On your feet Pavarotti!"

"We want to hear Miserere!"

As Daniel stood up and enveloped the room with song, his powerful operatic voice held his audience captivated.

Even though the lyrics were sung in Italian, young and old were consumed by emotion.

The English translation speaks to every soul —to answer the question: *"What makes us who we are?"*

The song *Miserere* translates into English as *Have Mercy*.

Have mercy, have mercy,

Have mercy, poor me.

But I drink to life!

What a misery is my life

What a misery!

I'm a sinner of the year eighty thousand

A liar!

But, where am I? And what do I do?

How do I live?

I live in the soul of the world

Lost in the depths of life!

Have mercy, poor me.

But I drink to life!

I'm the saint who betrayed you

When you were alone

And I live elsewhere and I look at the world

from the sky

And I look at the sea and the woods

I see me ... living in the soul of the world

Lost in the depths of life!

Have mercy, poor me.

But I drink to life!

If there was a night dark enough

to hide myself, hide myself

If there is a light, a hope

Gorgeous sun shining

inside me

Give me the joy of living
that isn't still here
Have mercy, have mercy,
That joy of living
that maybe it is not still here.

The evening's entertainment continued but no one could shake the message of the opening act.

The dining hall was quickly restored to its formal setting. Cheerful goodbyes sent the residents of the Beit Nir Kibbutz to their respective houses.

The five friends walked along the cobbled stone path, each deep in thought. Their individual response to what happened at the bring-and-share party was unexpected. Although they were tired it was too early for bed. They nestled in the comfortable couches and lounge chairs, wrestling with an avalanche of reflections.

Connor broke the silence.

"Humanity needs a spiritual awakening in order to move toward the rebirth of a better path," he reflected.

"The deepest form of despair is for man to choose to be something other than himself."

A hesitation to respond alluded to the fact that the friends were embarking on territory they had little or no knowledge of or experience in. Presuming to know what action would save the human race would be audacious.

"The locus of change must start within ourselves if we are

to make a positive impact on the world around us; we have to first accept blame for our own failures," said Jon, thinking of his parents' bad decisions at home.

"Exactly, but change can be difficult. We're conditioned to accept the results of our decisions, good or bad, as chance, luck, or fate, or simply beyond our control," responded Emma.

"Kids our age are lured into thinking that the purpose of life equals upward social mobility, establishing a career, accumulating wealth, competing and holding power," said Lea.

"And even if we aren't content with the trappings of success, we tend to cling to these illusions because they're all we know," she continued.

"Here's what I'd like to propose: maybe our purpose has nothing to do with what we end up doing for a living, when our purpose is really about living authentically and discovering who we really are," commented Connor.

"Remember the Bible verse on the poster at the camp we went to, that trials and tribulations throughout our lives should be welcomed with all joy," he added.

"The message has stayed with me; whenever things get tough I'm reminded that obstacles are put on our path to help us determine if our heart actions will result in gold, silver and precious stones that can be refined and last the test of time, or if we opt for choices that will result in wood, hay and straw that can easily be diminished and are short-lived ..." said Jon.

"Individuals are taught from a young age to look to others for guidance, but problems step in when kids grow up and questions about life's purpose remain unanswered," said Connor.

"Society has opted to fit GenZ into a slot that makes more sense for them, basically to persuade us to continually deny who we are," said Lea.

"I guess it's easier to copycat the familiar, instead of upsetting the apple cart," Jon said.

"Do we chase money by seeking a lucrative career or do we follow a strong inner impulse accompanied by conviction of divine influence?" Emma intervened.

"What you're referring to is a calling. It starts as a hunch then swells into a compulsion that you just can't shake," said Lea.

"A calling isn't an easy path, which is why most people ignore it. They fear the unknown and the risk of being perceived as foolish," she continued. Emma nodded, thinking of the day she decided she wanted to be a chef.

"Most people prefer to adhere to the status quo. Society has reduced the human lifecycle to a list of boxes to be ticked: graduate from school, get a degree, get married, start a family, settle into a well-defined career path, and hang on until retirement check scan be collected," Zach weighed in.

"My parents are a good example of this; and are they fulfilled? I don't think so!" Jon added.

"This well-worn path pushes people in the direction of conformity, not purpose," said Zach.

"We're so busy avoiding self-induced fears of not being

smart enough, creative enough, pretty enough, that we rarely stop and ask "How should I go about changing things?" added Emma.

"On that topic, just how should our generation initiate constructive change?" Connor prompted.

"We live in a society that does not value silence, instead it values action. All the joy we crave is within, but the world today is like a man who has locked his vast riches in an impenetrable vault but who has no idea where the key is," Zach suddenly said, reflecting on his own behavior.

"Living without silence is dangerous; without it you end up believing that you, and all that you aspire to, is your sole purpose," said Lea.

"Does that mean people are controlled by their dark side," Jon asked.

"Carl Jung apparently called it 'the shadow', the underbelly of one's personality that represents our deficiencies, failures, and selfish urges," Lea answered.

"Ironically, the part of you that's darkest has the most to teach you about your purpose. It shows you from whom you most need to learn ... it's usually the people you like least who have the most to teach you about yourself," she elaborated.

"This is why most people live out their lives having never known their true purpose."

"So what you're saying is, we need to wise up and be the heroes in our own lives," Zach stated.

"Exactly! The poor as well as the rich are crouched at the

starting line of a new and startlingly different race into the future. There is a great need today for what can best be termed a consciousness of the future, yet if we are to survive this journey it is incumbent upon us to supplant the old, unworkable thought patterns with new ways of thinking before those old ways capture and destroy us," Lea continued.

"Every age has had its future and its dream. The traditional world is collapsing," Zach agreed.

"Superman is too busy! We're going to have to do it for ourselves, no apologies or excuses," stated Connor to a titter of laughs from the group.

"Let's face it, Superman or some other fictional character isn't coming to save mankind, ever, because they are not real!" said Emma.

"The good news is that we don't need them. Simply put, we need to be the heroes in our own lives," Lea reminded them.

"That makes perfect sense. The person with the most influence over our thoughts, words, decisions and actions, even when we make mistakes or experience failure, will always be the reflection looking back at us in the bathroom mirror every morning," Jon responded.

"Being our own hero must surely be difficult!" Zach prompted.

"Unfortunately there's nothing easy about being the hero in your own life story. It means having to take full responsibility for all your actions. If you drink too much, you're going to mess up somehow. If you don't work hard on school assignments you will get poor grades and jeopardize your chances of acceptance at a good university or college … the list goes on!"

Her words had a serious message to them but she smiled warmly at her circle of friends as she spoke.

"We must also stop making excuses and blaming others for our problems," Lea said.

"For centuries humans have asked the question, "Why am I here?" Although we have never found a definitive answer to this question it does not stop us from searching. People generally believe the question is linked to religious explanations but some view it more as a desire to understand our general purpose in life."

"Perhaps it's enough to know that a Creator created us for His pleasure and purpose, even if we don't know exactly what the pleasure and purpose entails," said Zach.

"This remains a mystery, to be revealed beyond the grave," he continued.

"Humanity seeks leaders to provide an answer to this question, to help them identify, understand and refine their role on Earth," countered Jon.

"It's more a question of seeking ways to better understand the fundamental principles of life, our natural need for survival, purpose and achievement," said Emma.

"Humans have always looked for people to follow, learn from and be inspired by," agreed Lea.

"Hero-seeking is such a part of our collective, modern-day

DNA," said Zach.

"It's important not to trivialize the concept of being a hero ourselves," he continued.

"I loved reading comic books as a young child, and grew up believing I could be a hero like Spider-Man, Captain America and Iron Man or Superman, Batman and Green Lantern. I actually imagined pulling people to safety, putting out forest fires, preventing wars from destroying countries. I wanted to be a hero; who doesn't?" admitted Connor.

"People have tagged on to the next best thing … they've become obsessed with celebrities, bordering on being abnormally obsessive; behavioral change includes anxiety, fear, depression, envy, frustration, and rejection," said Emma in agreement.

"As teens it's natural to seek positive role models we can emulate. I find comfort in reading about famous and popular people in our culture who suffer similar woes to our own … they dress badly, they miss opportunities and get into arguments just like the rest of us," laughed Lea.

"But can people change by adopting a growth mindset?" Jon intervened.

"I believe so; a growth mindset believes anything is possible. We can all change, grow and improve," said Zach.

"Knock-Knock."

"Who's there?"

"Opportunity!"

"Don't be silly, opportunity doesn't knock twice!

"Okay, I get it."

"One of the most beautiful things is when you find your own way, something uniquely special that you are good at, that you love doing. It makes answering questions like: 'What is life asking of me?' and 'What will give my life meaning and purpose?' easier. In short, ask 'What is my conscience directing me to do?'" Lea said.

"My conscience is telling me to hit the sack," Jon remarked.

Jon, Lea, Zach, Connor and Emma marched in single file to the bathroom door, where they stood quietly waiting as each took a 2-minute turn to brush their teeth. Jon came out first.

"Bus 011 runs from Kiryat Gat tomorrow afternoon, leaving at 3 pm. It will take us 15km east to visit the ruins of the ancient city of Mareshah, burial caves, agricultural facilities, and an amphitheater. Stories about the history of the caves would be a worthwhile lesson to contemplate the meaning of existence. It is a holy site to Christians, Jews, Druze and Muslims," he said, walking toward the communal dormitory shared by the boys.

Chapter III

Road of Trials

The site hosted the remains of Mareshah, an ancient city, as well as a series of man-made caves in the underground limestone. Some of them had painted murals from over 2000 years ago. Others were carved in the shape of a bell. History had been played out at the site, which had remains from the Edomites, Greeks, Romans, Jews, Muslims, early Christians and Crusaders. There was also a large cemetery, amphitheater and architectural remains from the Roman and Byzantine periods to be seen. A tour guide ushered in small groups of tourists.

"Most of the bell caves were dug during the Early Muslim period."

"Finds from the Crusader period indicate that Mareshah had functioned as a small city."

"In the sixth century, as a result of Zedekiah's rebellion against the Babylonian kingdom and its king Nebuchadnezzar II, the latter occupied the Judean kingdom and sent many of its inhabitants into exile."

"This marked the end of Mareshah as a Hebrew city."

Emma and Jon deviated from the tour group. They had noticed armed guards patrolling the area, inspecting parked vehicles. The driver of the tour bus that had brought them to the site was nowhere to be seen.

After the passengers disembarked at the entrance of the caves, the bus driver had driven on toward a makeshift parking lot a short distance from the historical site.

Shade was at a premium but he had spotted a rudimentary open structure with a roof covering made from remnants of frayed cloth, further along. It was still early; the return trip was scheduled only for five o'clock.

Zach gestured wildly for Jon and Emma to return to the tour group. His face was stricken. It looked like he had seen a ghost.

Mere minutes ago a monotonous whirring noise had alerted his attention. The same sound caused the security personnel to scatter and seek the source of the uninterrupted drone that sounded like a defective engine.

Instinctively Zach moved in the direction of the commotion. The sight of the overturned bus overwhelmed his imagination.

How was it possible to overturn the bus on a road that was flat and free of any obstacles? It was very hot; he worried if the driver had suffered heat stroke and passed out.

As Zach approached the front of the vehicle he witnessed the terrified bus driver shielding his head from a hail of stones. A rock strategically hit the man above his eye, instantly rendering him blind as blood covered his eyes and face.

His attackers were unperturbed at the consequence of their attack and aggressively pelted the old man with small rocks until he fell backwards.

Still shielding his head and face, he pleaded for them to stop but each of his aggressors kicked him until he lay motionless. His face and arms were caked with blood and sand.

The four hooligans repeated a word that Zach did not recognize, although he surmised it to be derogatory, for they had clearly targeted their victim deliberately.

They were caught by surprise when the guards grabbed hold of them and handcuffed them. Zach hid at the rear of the vehicle, mesmerized by the gruesome incident that had just occurred. It was eerie. The engine of the bus was struggling to recover in the same way as the injured bus driver: in fits and starts. Zach thought the driver must be dead. He lay motionless.

A guard cut the engine by removing the key from the ignition while another attended to the injured man. After feeling for a pulse the guard indicated to his colleagues that he victim was breathing. The voice of the tour guide could be heard as she called the sightseers to an adjacent cave.

Seconds later the terrorist gang was marched a distance from the historic site. They offered no resistance, but nodded in approval as they observed the state of their victim; they had accomplished what they had set out to do. Zach made a quick departure.

"Our bus driver was seriously injured shortly after we got here. The bus was struck by stones thrown by Palestinian youths. He lost control of the vehicle and crashed. I'm not sure if he'll make it; he looks pretty beat up. Four Palestinian youths were arrested."

The tranquil atmosphere suddenly exploded into chaos for a second time within minutes, although the rest of the tour group was blissfully unaware of the first terrorist attack.

A man dressed in black emerged from one of the caves, his head and neck was camouflaged by a *keffiyeh* scarf. He opened fire on the tourists, narrowly missing the unsuspecting tour guide.

When the individual saw the armed guards, he attempted to flee the scene but was shot in the leg by a member of the Israeli security personnel. Mayhem erupted. The report of the two separate incidents, first the brutal stoning followed by an attempted assassination, was radioed in and a helicopter was summoned. It was then that Zach and Jon became the center of attention.

The guards gestured to where the boys were standing. Both boys were wearing *keffiyeh* scarves they had bought online before arriving in Israel. The distinctive checkered black and white scarf was a fashion statement back home. Little did they know the *keffiyeh* had become a symbol of Palestinian nationalism, an icon of Palestinian solidarity.

The two teenagers were flung to the ground, their hands handcuffed behind their back, and pulled to their feet. It all happened so fast their minds were slow to react. The helicopter landed a short distance off, raising a cloud of swirling dust.

Neither Jon nor Zach protested as the Israeli Security personnel manhandled them into the helicopter. They were too scared to put up a fight.

Logic prevailed that they would be given the opportunity to sort out this obvious misunderstanding.

Next, the four hooligans who had caused the bus driver to

overturn the vehicle were pushed aboard the aircraft. Two stretchers, respectively carrying the shooter and the bus driver were crammed on to the center of the floor space.

"*Let's go!*" one of the security guards shouted.

The boys stared in wide-eyed horror at the bloodied injured men. The four youths sat motionless, unperturbed at the haste in which their circumstances had changed from malicious intent to possibly being detained for years in an Israeli prison. Jon and Zach were later to learn that the shooter had a record of security-related offenses and had served time in prison before. Israeli Police confirmed that the man was a member of the Yeshiva.

The following day it was established that the four youths were sent by Hamas to intimidate the bus driver for allegedly being sympathetic to Israel's political struggle. The bus driver was a member of Fatah, a rival faction of Hamas.

Jon and Zach were locked in a holding cell for several hours, and interrogated until the early hours of the morning. They were believed to be left-wing activists.

Jon and Zach were moved to a detention center that looked like a compartmented aviary, made up of steel frame rooms with fine wire mesh for walls. The area offered no privacy, no seating, no toilet facilities, just concrete flooring.

Zach pointed to the security cameras, while Jon fixed his gaze on the occupants of the adjacent cage.

An old man in his 70s sat staring at the floor. His eyes seemed dead, like those of a man who knows he will never leave this place alive. A younger man, fitted with a false leg, smiled jauntily at the new inmates. Two other men stood at the far corner.

The four youths who had pelted the tour bus huddled near the entrance to the cage. Their hatred of anything Israeli was palpable. Their two week combat training at the Gaza camp the previous month had prepared them for the possibility of capture in enemy territory.

Jon noticed that one of the teenagers was a girl; he feared for the outcome if these kids were to be sentenced before an Israeli military court. But he also knew that these youngsters were highly skilled terrorists, experienced in weaponry and terrorist tactics. They were also fiercely patriotic and willing to sacrifice their lives for the Izz ad-Din al-Qassam Brigades, Hamas' military wing.

Jon had reason to feel strongly about prejudiced treatment of marginalized people, like the Palestinians. Jon's grandparents had suffered great injustices during South Africa's former Apartheid government.

Even now, in the situation he found himself in, Jon could not help but recognize that racial discrimination was rife the world over. Yet, apart from being as black-skinned as the Palestinian inmates, he had no repressed desire to join his brothers in arms in South Africa by fueling reverse-racism.

Jon liked to tell anyone who cared to listen that people in South Africa must 'get over Apartheid' by defeating its continued hold on people's psyches, and by ensuring economic liberation becomes a national obsession so that every citizen—irrespective of race, color or creed—may enjoy a comfortable, prosperous life.

He would stress his convictions that reverse racism, following the country's democracy in 1994, must not be construed as justified retribution for the national segregation associated with the Apartheid era. That previously disenfranchised people should resist flaunting a sense of entitlement, believing it is their right to be granted certain privileges based on the color of their skin.

He believed that they should instead adopt strength of character to triumph over adversity through increased efficiency. That the victim-syndrome is an excuse to avoid responsibility for their lives. That the present ANC government should desist from intentionally keeping the embers of Apartheid alive; as a powerful tool to unite certain parts of the population to incite violence in seeking retribution for every civil injustice.

Jon's balanced understanding of South Africa's political leadership had on many an occasion sparked skepticism and genuine unease about the country's future status.

He had become accustomed to answering questions that had often made him feel ashamed of his country's leadership.

"Why would your government want to keep racial disparity alive? Could it be so that younger generations do not forget their history, more precisely, the struggle previous generations had to endure to achieve freedom?" he had been asked.

"The negative connotations of Apartheid have become a convenient scapegoat for continued poor education and illiteracy, inadequate and corrupt service delivery, unemployment, crime, and poverty in the country. While Affirmative Action in the mid-1990s was introduced as a way of making the workplace more representative and fair, this policy today excludes white jobseekers from competing for equal job opportunities with black, colored and Indian people. It is common knowledge that the ANC is systematically forcing white South Africans into poverty by banning them from workplaces. It is blatant racism," he would answer.

"If Apartheid was indeed the cause of the poverty of millions of South Africans, why are the citizens in most other African countries generally even poorer, despite the absence of Apartheid?" someone else had asked.

"I believe that even if Apartheid never happened, South Africa would be no different today. Institutional ineptitude and widespread bureaucratic corruption, alongside administrative inefficiency, are symptoms of institutional failure in South Africa and many African countries. It is an obvious observation, based on the long list of dictatorial leaders and undemocratic elections."

"Low growth rates, declining agricultural production, stagnating manufacturing, rising imports, and rapidly expanding external debts add to the poverty quotient, in addition to coups, civil unrests, ethnic violence, and widespread bureaucratic corruption alongside administrative inefficiency, and institutional ineptitude or outright failure." he continued.

"It's common knowledge that African leaders extract billions of dollars every year from their economically strapped countries, serving their personal needs and not those of their people. In my humble opinion, controlling or eliminating inept governance and corruption must begin with laying the foundation for strong institutions—economic, political, and social—in all sectors of the economy. I am dismayed at how things appear to have changed, but in reality remained the same. Only the faces of the people in charge are different, but the political game plan mirrors a familiar system that still persists in favoring racial dominance."

The general feedback he got, particularly from friends living abroad, was that society's real enemy is the forces of global capitalism, more so the predatory elite in the guise of bankers, governments and others who are driving their own nefarious agendas.

People's understanding of capitalism is often biased; many claim that the poor suffer because the rich are constantly increasing their wealth and using it to further oppress the poor.

It should be a driving force among the poor to rectify this disparity, yet what stands in the way is that while each person has equal rights to attain wealth, but unequal ability is to exploit those rights to the fullest. Some resort to enforced recognition, but no amount of compromise will make any person more able.

It occurred to Jon that governments devoted too much time and money on building barriers to prove their strength in battle, when they should be applying themselves to integrate allied nations and homelands if they hoped to stand any chance of peace and prosperity; fragmented alliances would put them at a disadvantage.

A perfect example was the South African government making the minorities, especially the white population, the 'enemy' and obstructing the way forward for his nation to thrive in harmony.

The detainees had no idea of the time; the detention center was permanently lit in bright artificial light, a technique to enforce insomnia. Although their circumstances did not resemble solitary confinement, Zach and Jon began to experience visual and auditory hallucinations and paranoia.

Jon, still unaware that the scarf around his neck prompted their arrest, proceeded to cover his head to shield his eyes from the invasive, bright light. This action did not go unnoticed; the guards were monitoring their every move on the surveillance camera.

Zach who was normally in control of his emotions displayed uncontrollable feelings of rage; the bright light burned his eyes.

In his annoyance of this turn of events he spread his scarf on the cold concrete floor as a place to sit.

Unwittingly his action demonstrated his disrespect for the symbol of Palestinian nationalism, which angered his fellow inmates in the adjacent cage.

One man grabbed hold of the wire mesh that separated Jon and Zach, violently shaking the partition. Judging by his tone of voice the language was no doubt unsavory. Another inmate threw his shoe against the wire partition. Jon had read somewhere that this gesture in Arabic culture is meant as an extreme insult.

Zach experienced distortions of time and perception; it was impossible to speculate how long they had been in this place.

Their wristwatches and mobile phones had been confiscated.

The girl in the next cage got up and faced the two boys in the next cage. Zach was apprehensive at first and did not know how to react to this young girl. He guessed her age to be about 12. She reminded him of his youngest sister back home in Texas. To their great surprise she spoke in English, albeit with a heavy accent.

"I am proud to be part of the al-Quds Army camp. These camps teach us about our Islamic sanctities that are being blatantly violated. They also strengthen our rights to defend our presence and resist the Israeli occupation," she explained.

Her face was stern. The expression in her eyes was devoid of emotion. But Zach and Jon were swayed by her conviction.

"But you are so young to be handling weapons," was Zach's feeble attempt to make conversation.

"What about your family? Will they not worry about you? Do they know you are being held captive in Israel?" Jon urged.

The young girl dismissed their questions with a wave of the hand and a flippant flick of the wrist.

"Women play a vital role in the future liberation battle. We learn about weapons and how to handle them, and we undergo intensive military training for this purpose."

She turned her back abruptly on the two foreigners, her body posture throwing off a storm of signals, and returned to her group. Her words of conviction impressed Zach and Jon, who recognized the importance of standing up for what you believe in.

"Standing up for your own rights, trusting your own instincts, braving the uphill battle to achieve your goals are some of the most important skills in life," said Zach.

"If you have strong convictions, people will always try to knock you down, but as long as you get back up, you're showing them that you can take a stance for what you believe in," Jon remarked.

"Come on, we must find a way to convince the Israeli Police that we are innocent!" Zach exclaimed.

"I'm worried how the two girls and Connor got back to the Kibbutz," Jon said.

"Hours of watching Discovery Channel's various survival series would hopefully have taught them the basics of staying alive in the desert."

As usual Zach tried to make light of the situation but this time, not even he believed the words coming out of his mouth.

"I don't think survival fantasies involving frog licking and urine drinking are typical challenges they might encounter!"

"Connor is a right Boy Scout, a true Kiwi farm boy!" Zach tried again.

"It's a demanding 15 km walk, and daytime temperatures drop to freezing at night." Jon wasn't comfortable right now, but he didn't like thinking about his friends lost in the desert.

The tourists at the historical site had dispersed in a hurry, following the stone throwing incident, shooting and aggressive capture of two teenage boys. Most of the tourists were Japanese, who were initially enthralled by the entertaining drama that played out, believing it to be a mock demonstration of Israeli Defense Force proficiency. But when they saw the bloodied casualties writhing in pain due to their injuries, they fled the scene in shock.

Within minutes the tour guide rallied the now frantic passengers on to the buses, hastily departing along the dirt road headed for Tel Aviv. The three forlorn teenagers were left stranded.

Emma, Lea and Connor stared at the long dirt road that led off to the Kibbutz. With no means of transport, they would have to rely on their wits to walk the 15km distance.

The sun was setting, and while it brought relief from the scorching heat of the day, it was a stark reminder that it would soon be dark, cold and hazardous.

Emma took a deep breath and pulled her shoulders back.

Nursing her mother through her illness and adjusting to life without her best friend when she died had made her resilient to most challenges and hardships.

It took determination and a lot of soul searching, but over time Emma had taught herself to smile even when faced with what seemed like insurmountable problems. She ran on the spot for a few minutes, exercising her arms and legs, like an athlete warming up for a big race.

"The only use of a challenge is for it to be conquered," Emma remarked.

Lea took her place alongside Emma.

"No worries. The desert doesn't scare me. I learned survival skills traveling the Australian outback with my brothers and father," Lea said.

"I'm glad you're both so chipper but we have to maintain control of our thoughts and emotions. We're not exactly armed with a survival kit," Connor cautioned.

"It's not the strength of the body that counts, but the strength of the spirit," Lea added.

Connor had the presence of mind to locate the abandoned overturned bus in search of food and items that might come in handy on their long walk.

"We had better get started. It will take us at least three hours to reach the compound."

The large area of arid rocky land was sparsely populated by Bedouin Arabs, camels and cacti.

On arrival, volunteers at the Kibbutz had been told that the desert beyond the compound was a dangerous place and the site of many violent clashes. They understood that it would be a disaster if one was to be stranded in the desert with no water, food or shelter.

Although no supplies of water or food were found on the

bus, self-protection was foremost in Connor's mind. He always carried a switchblade knife with him; he also retrieved a length of timber found in the bus, which he intended to carve into some sort of spear.

Lea produced a packet of crisps and Emma found a bar of chocolate in her backpack. But they had no water, which was a worry.

"We must be positive, I'll get you home safely," Connor said reassuringly.

The trio set off, walking side by side, using the road as their navigation guide. An hour later it was pitch dark. They could no longer see the road, but continued walking at a brisk pace.

No one complained about being tired, hungry or thirsty. The meager food supplies consumed earlier only intensified their unbearable thirst.

After walking non-stop for close on four hours Emma stumbled and landed on her knees. All three were exhausted.

They lay down calmly on the cold desert sand, their vigilance of possible predators having faded into the recesses of their minds.

The lure of sleep was blissful. Every fiber in their minds and bodies yearned for resurgence.

They were dehydrated and cold.

Only snacking on biscuits and an apple each before leaving the Kibbutz earlier that day, they were going into starvation mode. They had developed headaches and feelings of nausea.

Lea later recalled she had witnessed strange shadow-like

beings carrying her. These entities spoke a strange language, their voices echoing muffled sounds. She remembered seeing an orange glow in the distance, and that her head ached.

Connor related to Lea's visions; he described how he had tried to attack an unknown enemy but found himself incapable of even moving his arms. He remembered hearing himself utter deep guttural sounds like that of a wounded animal. He too recalled seeing an orange glow. Connor said that he thought he saw his sister at his side throughout the nightmarish trance.

Emma explained that her sleep had also been upsetting. She imagined that her body was engulfed in flames, and that hundreds of dead birds fell from the sky.

The three teens had mistakenly gone off the road and had walked for three hours into the desert.

But in their determination to reach the compound, even Lea with her knowledge of surviving in the Australian outback and Connor who had since junior school been a Boy Scout, failed to notice the change in landscape.

Connor's warning at the onset of their journey back to the Kibbutz was a stark reminder of how one's thoughts and emotions can become distorted under stress.

Both Lea and Connor later admitted to imagining looking to the night sky to determine the direction they should be taking, without a compass.

It was around midnight when they eventually stopped to rest. They knew they were lost, but too exhausted to plot an alternative route.

"Let us pray," Lea said.

The three friends knelt in a circle, held hands and bowed their heads.

"Dear Lord, we want to thank you for keeping us safe from the ordeals of this day. We are grateful for the opportunities to learn new things at the Kibbutz. We value the new friendships we've made. Lord, we humbly ask that You will protect Zach and Jon wherever they are, and return them to the Kibbutz unscathed. Lord, be our light in this darkness that we may find our way back safely to the compound. In Jesus' name we pray. Amen."

Not long after, a Bedouin family, camping in the desert, found them near their camel herd. It was fortunate that these desert dwellers brought Connor, Lea and Emma to the safety of their tent. A small fire inside made the tent warm and comfortable.

The teenagers were fed small quantities of water and covered with blankets for warmth. The friends were surprised the next morning, waking up in a traditional Bedouin tent, woven from goats' hair.

The family, comprising the father *Aamir*, mother *Altaf*, and twin boys, *Bachel* and *Hilel* sat staring at their guests.

The mother had prepared *Moraras*, pancakes made from flour, water, fat and honey. It was a very welcome meal.

At first communication was restricted to hand gestures and a lot of nodding and smiling. They did however recognize the name Beit Nir as a compound located several hours away by camel.

The father was conversant in broken English, having worked on an oil-rig in Saudi Arabia in his youth.

He told his guests that he and his family only camped out in the desert occasionally to teach their children the ways of their Nomadic forefathers. Their extended family lived in Oman.

"We live in the city of al-Sayyid, located in the Negev desert between Arad and Beersheba, just south of Hura," he explained.

Aamir saddled two camels and helped their guests climb on to the camels' backs.

The journey was an unusual experience. The view of the open plain was breathtaking. Connor steered the one camel, with Emma seated behind him, while Lea travelled with Aamir.

Altaf had provided ample nourishment for the journey, which consisted of dates, dried figs, yoghurt, nuts and cheese.

"*Hut-hut!*"Aamir commanded.

Immediately the camels started walking forward.

Connor held onto the reins but was careful not to tug the long-lines. He soon got the hang of the different commands, following by example of Aamir.

Gee was the command for turning right, *haw* for turning left, *whoa* for stop, *back* for backing up, and *hut-hut* for walking forward.

"As you give command 'gee', pull right long-line, which also instructs you to go right," Aamir explained in his broken English.

Connor had got so wrapped up in memorizing the verbal commands that he said "Cool" but the camel took it as "Koosh", which is an instruction to lie down.

Both Emma and Connor shrieked as their mode of transport came to an abrupt stop and proceeded to kneel on his front legs. Aamir found it hilarious. Connor praised the camel for her response by patting her gently on the neck.

"Hut-hut," he said.

"How long have you lived in the desert? Is it a hard life?" Connor asked.

"We don't stay one place too long; land ownership big problem. Big gaps between Bedouin culture and state culture."

"Is it true that many Bedouin women have 10 or more children each?" Emma enquired.

"Yes. Each woman is first, second, third or fourth wife, married according to Islamic Shari'a, to one man, living with him in one household."

"A big household must be expensive!" Lea remarked.

"It is. But a man is expected to marry more than one woman in order to prove his manhood. A man that has only one wife is thought to be weak and worthless."

"How do you earn so much money?" asked Connor.

"We get government welfare grants for every child, no matter is the mother married or single."

"So, bringing children into the world is a productive business," said Lea.

"Maybe, but many babies die!"

"What is the reason for this?" asked Emma, shocked.

"We marry our relatives. It is our way. So, many children born with health problems …"

"Do the Negev Bedouin now live in urban settlements?"

"Normal life today include modern houses, education, different jobs. Life is good. We have water, sanitation, electricity, also public institutions."

The group was silent as the camels moved on.

***

Zach and Jon heard a familiar voice. It was Daniel. He had contacted the Tour Operator who relayed the incidents to him, which brought him to the headquarters of the Special Police Unit tasked with crime fighting, maintaining public safety and counter-terrorism. Daniel had vouched for the boys' innocence and was given permission to return them to the Kibbutz. It was an exuberant reunion. The boys' appearance was disheveled, and they were starving.

"My cousin lives nearby. You can clean up at his place," Daniel offered.

Over lunch Daniel described the almost surreal sight of two camels approaching the compound. A man from the Bedouin tribe had brought Lea, Connor and Emma to the entrance gates of the compound.

Daniel described the sorry sight as the three teenagers literally fell from their respective camels' backs.

The three teenagers stumbled in, the worse for wear but grateful beyond words to be back.

Lea spontaneously hugged an old woman who happened to be walking by, saying that she missed folding bedsheets and would be back at work bright and early tomorrow morning.

Emma sprinted to the dining hall to make her apologies to Chef Shani.

Before Daniel could question Connor to hear what had happened to them, the girls were back.

It was difficult to make sense of their garbled rendition of what took place at the historic site of Mareshah; their versions were told in a faltering manner as if the three adventurers had suffered a life-changing ordeal. Daniel, on hearing that Zach and Jon had been arrested, immediately sped into action.

"So, here I am!" Daniel announced.

He pondered for a while, unsure how the boys would respond to his news, especially after the security police had been merciless in their cross-examination, withholding food and water, and depriving them of sleep.

"The Head of Police has invited us to a dinner this evening, to make amends for the misunderstanding. The event is an informal social gathering at a secret location, attended by influential leaders in politics, economics and human development."

The boys were excited at the prospect of listening to what these great minds had to contribute to finding solutions to the many complex problems in their country.

They wondered what, if anything, two 16-year olds from rural Texas and South Africa could possibly have to suggest that would make a difference.

Zach and Jon thought about the detainees they had seen at the Special Police Unit; how they might plead their cases.

The ride in an official vehicle was awesome until the driver accelerated to avoid a stampede of angry protesters.

Their chanting was deafening.

On closer inspection the occupants of the vehicle noticed that the activists, dressed in black from head to toe, were women. Their outcry resulted from an incident where a number of Palestinians, suspected of collaborating with Israel, had been executed by Hamas.

This retaliation happened a day after Israel allegedly killed three of the terror group's top military commanders in an airstrike in southern Gaza.

The driver, a security official, said the first batch involved 11 people who were killed in a shoot-out with city police, followed by six more in a public execution. Three suspected collaborators were also executed.

The victims, their heads covered and hands tied, were shot dead by masked gunmen dressed in black in front of a crowd of worshippers outside a mosque after prayers.

The boys were later to learn that Hamas had condemned the assassinations of the group's top military commanders, hence the protest by the women, calling it a 'big Israeli crime' for which the country would pay dearly.

Fighting intensified after Egyptian attempts to broker an end to the month-long war, with Palestinians firing dozens of rockets and Israel responding with airstrikes across Gaza.

The social gathering took place in a simple residence.

The mood was relatively subdued. The guests were on a strict time schedule, to exchange informal pleasantries and savor traditional cuisine before settling down to serious debate in preparation for a live broadcast within a fortnight.

The restrained ambiance was kicked up a notch when one particular conversation was heard above the humdrum monotones in the room.

"I'm reminded what Golda Meir, the fourth Israeli Prime Minister, said: We can forgive the Arabs for killing our children, but we cannot forgive them for forcing us to kill their children. We will only have peace with the Arabs when they love their children more than they hate us."

Jon moved closer to where the two men were standing.

"What is the history of Palestine, in a nutshell?" he asked.

"For centuries there was no conflict. In the 19th century the land of Palestine was inhabited by a multicultural population, mostly Muslim and a small minority of Hebrews. In the late 1800s a group in Europe known as Zionists, colonized Palestine to create a Jewish homeland, but the indigenous population resisted this notion. Fighting broke out, with escalating waves of violence. In 1947 the United Nations intervened, giving away more than half of Palestine to a Jewish state. Conflicts resulted in a spate of grisly massacres. Israel triumphed. Over 500 towns and villages had been obliterated. Three-quarters of a million Palestinians had been made refugees. In 1967 Israel conquered more land, following the Six Day War against Egypt. Israel finally occupied the West Bank and Gaza Strip,"

"What about the current conflict? Will Israel not be forever embattled occupying a small corner within a vast Muslim ocean?" Zach prompted.

"History moves on and you can't deny it or go back in time to change things. Benjamin Netanyahu, Prime Minister of Israel, put it succinctly: If the Arabs put down their weapons today, there would be no more violence. If the Jews put down their weapons today, there would be no more Israel."

"We will be slaughtered!"

"False propaganda is an unpredictable enemy. The truth about the Israeli-Palestinian conflict is often distorted by lies. For instance, Israel is not trying to change the status quo on the Temple Mount. In fact, over the course of a year 3-million Muslims visit the Temple Mount together with about 200 thousand Christians and 12 thousand Jews. Only Muslims are allowed to pray on the Mount; non-Muslims may only visit at specified times. Although the Temple Mount is Judaism's holiest site, where Solomon built his Temple 3-thousand years ago, Israel will not permit any change in the status quo. Instead, the ones trying to change the status quo are Palestinians, who are violently trying to prevent both Jews and Christians from even visiting the Temple Mount."

"Orthodox Jews pray facing Jerusalem and the Temple Mount, while Muslims pray towards the City of Mecca and Saudi Arabia. When they pray in Jerusalem they point their posterior to the Dome of the Rock and the Temple Mount."

"Palestinians use the Temple Mount as a playground, where they have picnics and play soccer. And from time to time they start riots on the Temple Mount; they even vandalize their own Mosque where the floor carpets are pelted with rocks and broken chairs."

"This behavior is disrespectful, which naturally fuels violent clashes between Orthodox Jews and Muslims!"

"The current violence is not the result of stagnation in the peace process. Israel experienced some of the worst terrorism in its history when the peace process was at its peak. The reason for Palestinian terrorism is neither progress nor stagnation in the peace process, but the desire of the terrorists to destroy Israel."

"The reason that conflict and violence persist is not because Palestinians don't have a state. They have repeatedly refused to accept a nation-state for themselves, if it means having to accept Jewish people living beside it. In 1937, the Palestinians rejected the Peel Commission report that called for two states for two peoples; in 1947, they rejected the U.N. partition plan that did the same. In 2000 at Camp David and again in 2008 the Palestinians rejected new proposals that would have created a Palestinian state. They rejected peace both before and after the creation of Israel, before Israel gained control of the territories in 1967 and after Israel vacated Gaza in 2005."

"Simply put, Palestinians have always been more concerned with destroying the Jewish state than with creating a state of their own. The core of the conflict remains their persistent refusal to recognize the nation-state of the Jewish people."

A mixture of raucous laughter filled the room. Daniel, Zach and Jon turned their attention to a group seated in the lounge.

"When I die, I want to go peacefully like my grandfather did, in his sleep; not screaming like the passengers in his car."

Daniel thought it a macabre joke, but found himself mildly amused. Without hesitation Jon offered a retort.

"For some, life is a fate worse than death," Jon exclaimed.

A man dressed in green fatigues extended his hand to greet the teenager.

Jon was aware that he had attracted an audience, waiting to hear his reason for exclaiming that some people's existence was deemed a fate worse than death. His retort had been incited by the statements made by the young Palestinian girl at the detention center.

Memories of conversations about segregation laws that were imposed by the South African National Party overheard as a young child between his parents and grandparents surfaced.

He never could comprehend the justification for prejudice and discrimination based on the color of your skin.

Jon was reminded daily of injustices that still persist today, injustices that go unpunished.

"I am a Zulu from South Africa. There are so many similarities between the Israeli-Palestinian conflict and that of South Africa's former ideology, the remnants of which still impact people's lives negatively despite the county's democracy more than two decades ago."

"In the early days of Apartheid my grandparents were forced to leave their traditional home to resume a new life in a separate African Reserve, known as a homeland."

"South Africa is a country blessed with an abundance of natural resources, including fertile farmlands and mines, but the plan with Apartheid to maintain white domination meant establishing racial territorial separation in regions that offered limited opportunity for advancement."

"Four homelands were established. Race laws touched every aspect of social life. All political rights were restricted. The creation of these homelands de-nationalized nine million citizens."

"You can't do that and not expect some major retaliation somewhere down the line. Protests resulted in imprisonment and assault. This pattern continued unabated for close on five decades, molding an entrenched inter-generational mindset of anger."

"Today the expectation of a better life is driven by demands made by people of all age groups, including older people who have not progressed in terms of education and material wealth. Kids my age have witnessed their grandparents and parents suffer the indignities of poverty, unemployment and poor living conditions."

"They're demanding that the government bridge the gap between the haves and have not's, wipe out poverty, create jobs, provide free education, build houses and remunerate the poor through welfare grants. Food shortage is a real challenge in most low-income households."

"The global perception might be that our country's transition in 1994 was peaceful and deemed a miracle considering its political history, but the international community should recognize that the velocity of arbitrary change taking place in South Africa is mostly chaotic."

"Even as a black person I believe people should put the past behind them and move forward. Politicians use the Apartheid legacy as a reason, or excuse, to halt progress."

"They are afraid if they work alongside whites or even share power they will be lose control of the country."

"The African Nationalist Congress wants it all but at what cost? South Africa, by all appearances is doing well, but there are massive problems that are conveniently being swept under the carpet. The media reports daily occurrences of farm murders, corruption, riots, strikes, crime and violence, which is steadily diminishing the country's political and economic structures."

"Today most citizens across the board accept racial prejudice, poor infrastructure, lack of services, and disruptive student activism as normal. Vast numbers of people can't find jobs. Poverty is rife. The poor have become dependent on welfare and Government grants to survive."

"South Africa is in trouble. It cannot afford to be a Welfare State and still hope to prosper as a developed country. This spiraling down pattern signifies a doomed nation."

"In other words, South Africa is a failed state!" affirmed Jon.

"So, you are saying that these crises persist today because remnants of the Apartheid regime are being kept artificially alive through unresolved anger, fear, retribution and rebellion, thus delaying the birth of a new cohesive South Africa."

'No country or nation can be built on discrimination,"

stated Jon with conviction.

"It is vital that leaders and the general public concede that meaningful contribution does not end with fault-finding or dredging up past atrocities. It requires every citizen to roll up their sleeves and tackle nation building for themselves."

"While the problems South Africa must contend with are mostly centered on cultural differences, the Israeli-Palestinian conflict is centered on religious differences, but also the issue of Palestinians claiming they are being driven off their land."

"In our defense, it was never their land. There is no country called Palestine. The original Palestinians were the Israelites. This conflict has everything to do with religion and the fact is Judaism has been around a lot longer than Islam. It was the Hebrews' land first."

"Islam was created in the 7th century, and the Israelites were there millennia before that!"

"People in Israel are fighting over our right to live in peace."

"For a nation to triumph over its past it must learn to act and think in a different way. It is often difficult to persuade people that a deep-seated belief has become obsolete, even damaging," proclaimed Jon.

The social gathering concluded with a sumptuous meal served in the dining room, after which the organizer of the event called delegates to convene the debate in preparation for a live broadcast that was to take place within a fortnight.

Daniel, Zach and Jon were escorted to a nearby airfield where a helicopter was waiting to take them back to the Kibbutz. The trip was unnerving; the driver switched off the headlights and drove stealthily in the blackness until he brought the vehicle to a standstill alongside the helicopter. The pilot hastily jostled the passengers aboard. The slow rotating sound of the exterior engine blade was a stark reminder for Jon and Zach of their frightening encounter with security personnel, leaving the ruins at Mareshah. They were grateful for Daniel's intervention, but their adventure was nothing short of a Hero's Journey. Every impulsive or orchestrated incident had tapped into their unconscious expectations, transforming dormant ideologies, losing their old selves, and emerging with renewed purpose.

The girls had prepared platters of cheese and olives. The five friends expressed their joy in an extended hug mingled with tears of joy.

"Our prayers have been answered."

Chapter IV

Heroes' Journey

Throughout history, wise people have advocated that in order to become a '(wo)man of knowledge' you must first conquer fear, recognizing that it is a treacherous enemy and often difficult to overcome. If you are terrified in its presence yet choose to remain passive, this enemy will have put an end to your quest. You will never learn. You will never become a '(wo)man of knowledge'. You will instead be timid, detached and defeated. Fear will succeed in manipulating your every thought and action. But if you absorb knowledge in the midst of fear, you will eventually conquer it. The defense is to be fully afraid and yet take the next step in learning, and the next, and the next. Finally, a moment will come when this enemy retreats, and you begin to feel sure of yourself. You become stronger. Learning is no longer a terrifying task. Clarity of mind is achieved. Your desires are known. Nothing is concealed.

Zach, Jon, Lea, Emma and Connor had taken the first amazing steps on the road to each becoming a '(wo)man of knowledge'. In their own unique ways they had conquered fear. They had learned important skills in survival. They had learned to question everything. They had learned never to give up. However, their experiences had uncovered more questions than answers. The friends welcomed the supposed serenity of their two-storey house at the Kibbutz. Things were ostensibly back to normal. The familiar sounds of the compound were reassuring, yet strangely unnerving.

The knowledge that anarchy prevailed in the country, that clandestine criminality reigned between opposing factions, that a terrorist attack, however minor, could disrupt the calm within seconds, was unsettling. The friends' recollection of petty terrorism had broadened their perspective of what a massive onslaught might look like. They knew they were vulnerable, unprepared. The aroma from the wild flowers in the garden permeated the central courtyard, which delighted their senses.

But the friends were alert to subtle nuances. They had noticed an increased military presence in the compound. And it was uncommon for the dining hall to be in darkness. Despite the imminent warning signs of an altered state of reality, they were comforted that their small circle was once again complete. Rachel had surprised them by dropping off a large bowl of *Acquacotta* soup for their supper.

"It's Italian peasant food," she added with obvious pride.

Emma gave Zach and Jon an impulsive hug.

"We were so worried about you guys."

"Likewise! Your ordeal in the desert and camel rides must have been great fun."

"Not!"

The shrill ear-piercing sound of an air-raid siren erupted the calm. Residents emerged from their homes and in an orderly fashion and hastily made their way to a designated shelter.

Numerous pre-cast concrete fortified square structures,

with colorfully decorated exterior walls, were permanent fixtures throughout the compound. The shelters were aboveground; fully-accessible structures. Daniel later explained that Operation Life-shield was an emergency campaign to save innocent lives. These steel-reinforced concrete shelters were in normal use as schools, kindergartens and senior citizen centers.

The five friends had made their way to a shelter hidden among the trees near their house. The mural depicted a beautiful landscape of rolling hills, green fields and horses drinking at a stream. It was impressive how quietly the residents had occupied the shelters. They had become accustomed to this kind of exercise over the years.

On previous emergency drills Israel had carried out more than 6 000 airstrikes, while Palestinian armed groups fired nearly 5 000 rockets and 1 800 mortars. But on this occasion the pre-emptive strike never materialized. Israeli jets had destroyed the enemy's rocket launching capabilities just minutes before it would have attacked the Kibbutz. As fellow residents exited the shelters to return to their houses, the five friends remained.

"Each of us experienced some sort of revelation with the recent trials we faced, and now this. Surely, this changes the way we should approach the future, showing people the way to strive for lasting peace?" Zach asked.

"Think about it for a moment. Today's world arises from a very different mindset. Some cultures even glorify hostilities and violent revenge as a solution," said Jon.

"But kids our age want to make the world a better place," added Emma.

"In order to achieve peace with justice, people's belief and perception of dispute and war needs to be changed," remarked Connor.

"No matter which direction one looks at war, it's a crime against humanity. The mindset is to kill people and destroy everything on a massive scale," added Lea.

"The world accepts that killing in war is legitimate, acceptable, and even glorious. Killers are given medals. Statues are erected in their honor to inspire future generations to follow by example," said Zach.

"What you're saying is that if our generation rejects war as a solution to political conflict, then the world will be moving towards peace with justice?" Emma asked.

"Certainly, but changing peoples' attitudes won't happen overnight. That alone will be a long struggle," commented Jon.

"It's not about leaving a better world for our children; it's about leaving better children for our world," said Lea.

"I suppose it's natural to look at the world from the comfort of our personal pulpit. You see it. You feel it. You know what must be done differently," Connor added.

"Someone has to take the lead, right? If not us, then who?" asked Lea.

"I believe everything starts with asking questions.

Everything is changing. We are changing. But are our values and objectives being adjusted to fit these new environments? asked Jon.

A tall well-built young man stood in the doorway of the concrete structure. He was dressed in track pants and a tee shirt. His head was partially shaven. He looked to be about 18.

"Hi. My name is Yossi. I'm the Krav Maga instructor."

"I've always wanted to learn self-defense!" exclaimed Zach.

"Can girls sign up?" Emma and Lea look at each other.

"Of course! Class starts tomorrow afternoon at 5 pm."

The friends walked back to their house. While the expectation of an imminent airstrike had a reflective effect on them, they were thankful disaster had been averted. What they did find disturbing was the submissive response of the other residents. In Judaism, based on the Torah, death is not a tragedy. It is a natural process. It is believed that our death, like our life, has meaning and is part of God's plan. However, life is valued above all else; taking a single life is like destroying the entire world.

Sleep came as a welcome relief. The fresh smell of clean linen, characterized by distinctive spicy-floral aromas of jasmine and bergamot, inspired peaceful dreams. Recent events had affected change in the way Zach would from now on collect newly-laid eggs and clean the chicken coops; the way Lea would sort, dry and fold laundry; the way Emma would peel the humble potato or chop an onion; the way Connor would grade the oranges and extract the golden liquid for bottling; and the way Jon would inspect the dairy cows for signs of illness, injury or distress.

Even though the volunteer work presented the same routine and expectations than before, each of the friends had undergone a perceptual shift in the way they identified with the tasks at hand. If ignorance was bliss before, awareness of becoming a '(wo)man of knowledge' was now paramount.

Zach, Lea, Jon, Connor and Emma accepted that from hereon they would have to journey through a challenging transition. They instinctively knew they would encounter considerable bewilderment as one way of life ended and an evolved mindset would take precedence to embrace new challenges. Start a new chapter as such. Or perish by the wayside. Escape was an illusion. Some kind of polarity was pulling their awareness in a different direction.

The friends had recognized qualities in Daniel they admired and they agreed to approach him to help them cross the threshold to developing their new conviction. The unfamiliar rules and values of their quest warranted mentoring.

Each of the friends had recently encountered major challenges and faced their greatest fear; death. Now that they were back at the Kibbutz, their individual pursuit was to nurture a new life at an elevated level.

Their heroes' journey had just begun. They were committed to finding the 'treasure' and bring it home.

The Krav Maga training took place in the school gymnasium. A training session was in progress. Several men and women were involved in intensive fighting that looked anything but simulated.

The new recruits later learned that these were trained soldiers. They were expert in carrying out disarms, striking and grappling tactics to escape from impossible situations.

"For the next two weeks you will learn moves that will become instinctive to your body."

"We need to be good at self-defense. The idea is to take our skills back home to teach others."

"We only teach Krav Maga to select individuals. The focus is anti-terrorism. Classes include fitness training, sparring, grappling, gun and knife disarms and dealing with suicide attackers. Exercises are acted out in real time against aggressive determined opponents."

"It sounds life-threatening. Hopefully we get to wear protective gear!" Zach joked.

"Krav Maga is the only martial art out there right now that was designed for survival purposes only. Anything that we teach is designed for self-defense and self-preservation. We follow no rules. We don't prepare ourselves for competition or tournaments. Practitioners spend their entire training time preparing for war. All Krav Maga techniques are designed for self-defense in a realistic street environment situation."

Introduction to Krav Maga started with the 'muay', a front kick drilling with both rear leg and front leg, the side-kick and the knee kick. This was followed by some striking drills using the elbow, basic punching and blocking. As the daily lessons progressed, the trainees learned to combine elements of blocking, punching, kicking and take-downs.

"The next stage of the training will cover hand grabs, shirt grabs, and chokes."

The group responded instinctively to ground compliance techniques and rapid destruction techniques, as well as moves to defend against knife threats and attacks. They also trained with improvised weapons such as jackets, belts and key chains.

"The kickboxing fights are extreme," remarked Connor.

"It helps that we are fit," Jon shot back.

"Next we will move on to knife threats, then knife attacks."

Yossi taught them how to deal with every sort of attack from every possible angle, close range and from a bit of a distance, as well as gun threats from every possible direction and angle.

The trainees were by now at the peak of their fitness, and were ready to be exposed to hand-to-hand combat.

"Today we will deal with situations when you are pushed against a wall, attacked with a knife, stick or gun—essential skills in anti-rape and hostage situations."

Yossi had asked a group of trained Israeli soldiers to interact with the newly qualified Krav Maga practitioners. The fights that ensued were full force and as real as any impromptu assault. The lessons learned were put to good effect. It was evident that their moves were swift and instinctive. Even the trained soldiers were impressed.

"Yossi, can you explain the origin of Krav Maga?" asked Connor.

"Krav Maga training is all about the real world. When people train in boxing or martial arts such as Jujitsu or Karate they sometimes wonder, But what about the real world? Would this training really help me on the

street?' Krav Maga is a combination of boxing and several martial art disciplines."

"Krav Maga also borrows techniques from Aikido, Judo and wrestling, along with realistic fight training."

"But how did Krav Maga develop?" asked Lea.

"Initially it was derived from street-fighting skills as far back as mid-1930s. The system was improved over time and became known in Israel as Krav Maga. Elite security guards of Jerusalem were trained in gun disarms and knife defenses. These guys fought for a living, in the meanest streets of Jerusalem. Their opponents were knife wielding assassins, drunken thugs, and suicide bombers. Just to be accepted as a guard one had to have served in a combat unit in the Israel Defense Forces. Many of them also had served in the Russian army. The qualities they needed to develop included technique, awareness, discipline and aggressiveness, and the ability to improvise, adapt and survive."

"I bet they also had to learn to deal with pain!" commented Emma.

"It was created so that Jews without any weapons, or any other resources for that matter, could defend themselves."

"It's always better to be prepared and to prevent something from happening than healing it afterwards."

"Krav Maga is about real fighting in action, not simply a display of technique."

"You are graded according to technique, discipline, and aggressiveness. Technique is obviously important. Discipline pertains to following rules and regulations so the job will be done effectively and by strict guidelines. Aggressiveness is vitally important."

The two-week intensive training came to an end. Yossi had expressed his approval of his new graduates. He cautioned them however not to flaunt their capabilities, but to apply their knowledge of self-defense and survival skills intelligently. Yossi stated that every person, young and old, should learn at least the basics of self-defense, and that it would be a good thing for the friends to share their knowledge as Krav Maga trainers in their own country.

Daniel had become a constant spectator at the gymnasium over the friends' two-week training period. He had got to know Connor, Lea, Zach, Jon and Emma well in a relatively short time, since their arrival at the Kibbutz. They had confided in him on many occasions that they believed him to be the right person to mentor them about life and how to find solutions to perennial problems burdening humanity. But mostly, they wanted to know how they could discover their true purpose in life. He responded to their enquiries on a variety of issues at length.

"Most people today are unhappy with the world they live in. Young people are especially angry because they will be left with the responsibility of having to restore the planet, somehow."

"Past generations exploited the Earth for profit. The effects of climate change are accelerating the extinction of animal species. The earth's land mass is receding. Coasts are sensitive to sea level rise and warmer ocean temperatures."

"Rising atmospheric concentrations of carbon dioxide are causing the oceans to absorb more of the gas and become more acidic."

"Even cultural values worldwide are rapidly being eroded. Wars resulting from differences in ideologies threaten to bring humanity to the point of extinction."

"World famine is a looming threat. By now most of us have heard the forecast that there will be 9.2 billion people in the world by 2050, but current projections suggest human numbers will not stop there. They will keep on climbing to at least 11.4 billion by the mid-2060s."

"What will the world of tomorrow be like?"

"Millions of discarded mobile phones and other electronic devices are being dumped illegally in developing countries. The global volume of electronic waste increases annually."

"The extent of electronic waste is about 7kg for every person on the planet. That's massive!"

"Because electronic goods contain toxic substances such as lead, mercury, cadmium, arsenic and flame retardants, once dumped in landfills, these toxic materials seep into the environment, contaminating land, water and the air."

"And it's causing serious health problems to people who live in these landfill countries."

"Another huge problem today is that many young people have no direction. They are struggling to make the leap into adulthood, as educators, leaders and as parents."

"And what about religion? Today's kids are moving away from religion."

"Religion has become a dirty word. Even talking about religion makes most people uncomfortable."

"Perhaps people should look at the meaning of the word. The word

religion comes from the Latin 'religio', which means 'to bind together'. According to scripture, that's essentially its purpose, to unite the human race and to foster the spirit of love and fellowship amongst men."

"Then why is religion central to conflict—war and terror attacks?"

"Religious fanaticism is on the rise."

"Young people particularly are being swept up by these ideologies. They are keen participants because they believe it will give them a personal identity. Young people have a powerful need to belong."

"A lot of people today live well below the poverty line. Many don't have much of an education. They can't find jobs. On top of that, many kids come from broken families. They live in rough neighborhoods, which are the breeding grounds for street gangs, drug abuse and violence."

"Young people are right to be angry. They want a better life. And when their circumstances don't show any likelihood of improvement they usually release their anger in some form of violent behavior."

"Even pre-teens suffer from depression and feelings of hopelessness. So, when a gang or a fanatical ideology promises them a so-called life of purpose, they are easily influenced."

"Also, rapid changes in third world countries are a motivating factor. Young people especially are attracted to religious ideologies that offer them freedom, new skills and the opportunity to connect with like-minded groups."

"They hate that their disadvantaged governments accept economic and political support from wealthy nations in the West, especially since they perceive their sponsors' culture as decadent and irreligious."

"This strengthens the hand of fanatical religious leaders."

"Many oppressed people worldwide, particularly religious fanatics,

believe that socialist revolution offers the way out of their misery. Terror attacks against secular forces and governments are rife.

"Ironically, humanity today is spiritually rudderless."

"The world is constantly at war. You would think history would have taught nations that in war everyone loses. Even the side that triumphs would have suffered great losses!"

"Sixty million people have been displaced by the current wars; the highest number of uprooted since World War II."

"Nobody really does anything to change these atrocities from recurring. The world responds with disturbing paralysis."

"Things are worse than they've been in a long time!"

"Instability is spreading. Suffering is growing. No country remains untouched."

"There are deeper forces at work in today's world. There is an agenda to reduce the world population that we are not privy to."

"The world trembles at what may be the dawn of World War III."

"People have become lazy. They sit back and wait for someone else to put out the fires."

"Or, they are brainwashed! What will it take to wake them from their stupor?"

"Riots and protests have become the order of the day. Violence is believed to be a great persuader!"

"A tight rein on people's personal finances is a sure way of keeping the masses under control. People fear poverty above all else!"

"There is already so much poverty in this world; it's hard to imagine a surefire way to empower families to escape its grip."

"Poverty, as many believe, is not a natural phenomenon. It is entirely

manmade and can easily be overcome by the actions of human beings."

"I disagree. Rather it's wealth that is manmade. Poverty is caused by war and political instability, social inequality, poor education, overpopulation, vulnerability to natural disasters, and epidemic diseases."

"All of which are manmade!"

Daniel, despite only being in his mid-20s, had more life experience that most people in their 60s. Prior to making Israel his home he had lived in Poland with his parents. But when elections in post-war Poland sparked off a succession of anti-communist revolutions across Eastern Europe, his parents left the 3-year old boy to live in the country with his grandmother. Here the child would be safe, they surmised. He thrived for about two years until the sudden death of the old woman. Milosz, as he was called then, had to learn to survive on his own. He begged for food on the streets. He would sleep in abandoned buildings. Children threw stones at him. Dogs attacked him.

On entering a village he met an old peasant woman who gave him food and lodging. But it soon became clear to young Milosz that his new ward had ulterior motives. He was forced to work long hours in the fields, clean the pig pens and chop wood. She would beat him with a stick if he fell asleep before finishing his chores. As punishment he often went without food for days. Once he tried to run away, but she tied a long rope around his ankle to prevent any future attempts. Even at night, he was chained to his bed.

This torturous existence continued until the child turned

ten. He was emaciated and filthy. His hair was matted. He never spoke. His unkempt appearance invited cruel name-calling from the other villagers. The only way he knew to lighten his hard existence was to sing a prayer his grandmother had taught him.

A travelling merchant visiting the village heard the boy sing as he shoveled muck from the pig pens. The merchant paid the old peasant woman in pots and pans to take the boy off her hands. Milosz was elated. His new 'foster parent' saw that he got cleaned up. He gave him clean clothes and regular meals.

But Milosz was soon to discover the reason behind this generous charity. He was made to beg on the streets of Warsaw, attracting attention by singing folk songs the merchant had taught him.

The young boy was in awe of the Gothic churches and neoclassical palaces. He had never seen modern skyscrapers and so many people in all his life. Warsaw had a thriving nightlife and music scene. Milosz would spend hours listening to operatic recitals. He had become a familiar figure at these venues and eventually came and went as he pleased. The performers were very kind to the frail boy with the voice of an angel.

The musicians welcomed him into their fold, coaching him in the classic genre. At last the teenager had found a home where he could live a decent life. Soon thereafter, the travelling merchant was arrested and put in jail for stealing a horse. Milosz was free at last. He spent hours at the public library, and was an avid reader. His knowledge of religion, cultures and countries even impressed learned scholars.

Milosz learned about Jesus and that He was a Teacher of the Truth. This revelation put Milosz on a path toward his true purpose in life. He wanted to follow the same vocation as Jesus. Although his upbringing had nominally been Roman Catholic, he became an avid student of the Bible whilst in Warsaw. Eventually he saved enough money from the many odd jobs he held in the neighborhood to buy a one-way passage from Warsaw to Tel Aviv.

On his arrival he befriended an Israeli couple who saw the qualities of an exceptional human being in him. At first he worked in their general store stocking shelves but after a few years the husband and wife decided to adopt Milosz as their son. His name was changed to Daniel. His time with them he counted as a blessing.

Daniel had listened patiently as the five teenagers voiced their opinions of what was wrong with the world.

"Are you ready to lead the journey of a lifetime?" Daniel asked.

"Someone once said, 'A journey of a thousand miles must begin with a single step,'" said Emma.

"The big question is 'What is necessary that we may ultimately achieve our goal to endorse our purpose in life?'" Daniel enquired.

"We know that we are only 16. But ignorance and inexperience is not an excuse, nor should it be an obstacle. We must start our journey now or we might miss out on some really amazing things that life has to offer," Zach conceded.

"We can take the lessons that we have learned in life so far and the experiences that we have gained from it and move on," noted Emma.

"It is because of the heartaches, as well as the hardships, that help to make us stronger people in the end," remarked Connor to Emma.

"People come and go throughout our lives, but sometimes we are lucky to meet exceptional people who will stay in our hearts forever, no matter what. The lessons that we learn from them will stay with us forever," Jon said, looking at the friends around him.

"Life is a journey filled with lessons, hardships, celebrations and special moments that shape our purpose in life. The road will not always be smooth, but the many challenges you encounter along the way will test your courage, strengths, weaknesses and faith," Daniel remarked.

"In other words, obstacles are really blessings in disguise, even if we don't recognize them at the time!" said Emma.

"The Bible says those who are saved, or born again, should count their trials and tribulations as joy... testing of one's faith produces perseverance, which in turn makes one mature and complete, not lacking anything," Zach said to Daniel.

"I guess how we react to problems determines what the rest of our journey through life will be like," said Jon.

"Things won't always turn out the way we want them to. I

suppose it's a matter of accepting temporary setbacks and finding out where we went wrong, and what it is we still need to learn," he continued.

"Positive experiences are priceless. They motivate us to continue our journey to discover what life has in store for us," commented Lea.

"It is also our aim to help kids our age to look inside themselves in order to find a whole, different person that they never knew existed," she said to Daniel.

"Even so, people can give you advice on how you should live your life, but essentially each person must do what they believe is right," she finished.

"It's important to be yourself. Not to be afraid to have an opinion. Say what you want to say. Do what you want to do," Daniel said, smiling at the teenagers before him. He was proud of the growth he had witnessed taking place in each of them.

"It's often said that what doesn't kill you will make you stronger. It's reassuring to compare the person you were before to the person you've become because you chose a different route," Jon stated.

"Everything that happens in our life happens for a reason. Think of it as a life lesson. Learn from it," Jon finished, nodding at his friends.

"On this journey, it doesn't matter what specific actions you take or skills you learn to make the world a better place. What matters is the bigger purpose, becoming bigger than yourself. Once you do, you will recognize your purpose in life,"

Daniel interrupted.

"Sounds great, but taking that leap to deepen your knowledge isn't as easy as just saying, 'Let it be so'. It will take a lot of work," Zach commented.

"I suppose, we must first recognize our strengths and weaknesses. Whenever we're confronted with a challenge that fits our capabilities, we need to comply with due diligence. But when we're frustrated, fearful, wishing people would be different ... we need to take a giant leap to expand our heart and mind?" he continued looking at Daniel.

"Exactly! It's important to see the bigger picture. Feel what others must be feeling. Put yourself in their position. Understand. Don't condemn. Don't judge. Try to grasp what lies behind the things people say and do. It helps if you have some idea of their background, what adversity they've endured, and in what way their past impacts their current and future circumstances.

Encourage them to reveal their problems, and their aspirations.

Guide them to look beyond the immediate crises. Outline proposed outcomes to test the feasibility of realistic solutions ... this will help make informed choices whether to accept, change or walk away from certain options.

If others react badly to your well-intended intervention, realize that it's not about you, but about their anguish," Daniel said.

"So, it's important to wish others well even if they are unreceptive to advice?" asked Connor.

"Consider how you can help lessen their suffering. Often it's wise not to get involved. Sometimes it's just by paying attention, listening to their complaints. Other times you need to lend a hand. Bear in mind, you don't need to take over and solve everyone's problems. They probably don't want that. Often just being there for moral support, a sympathetic ear, can improve peoples' lives. Do something to make them smile. Compliment them on something they are doing for themselves to improve their plight. Help someone tidy their home, or show them how to start a vegetable garden. Make them a meal. Give them an article of clothing they need," Daniel explained.

"In other words, we must appreciate that the life we've been given is a gift. We must make the most of it, and not waste a second," commented Emma.

"It is fulfilling to make the lives of others a little better," agreed Lea.

"Yes, helping others is a very noble gesture. Mother Teresa devoted her life to caring for the sick and the poor, working in the slums of Calcutta until her death at the age of 87," said Connor.

"It appears that many celebrities today are ambassadors of welfare organizations that provide financial aid to help sustain impoverished communities," added Zach.

"However, Christ came to serve and help others; not Himself. In fact, so much so that He laid down His life for others; not just for decent and moral people, but even for the worst of the worst such as murderers, adulterers, thieves and suchlike. He paid the ultimate price," he continued.

"Finding one's purpose is a very individual path. Only you can actually know it or figure it out. You are responsible for your own walk on this Earth," Daniel said to the group.

"The Bible is also known in certain quarters as Basic Instructions Before Leaving Earth, or life's instruction manual, where your walk is clearly governed by a higher Power, who has each person's very essence, or soul, at heart, preparing one for an eternal life after the short one here on Earth," said Jon.

"Living one's purpose typically unfolds in mysterious and surprising ways. It's not something that can be forced. I like to think of it as a journey of self-discovery, whether it's through meditation, self-talk or listening to the counsel of others," Daniel replied.

"Or going on a journey of moral or spiritual significance. We came to Israel for a simple working holiday, which has given us so much more!" Lea exclaimed.

"It's a matter of taking whatever steps or inspiration call to you. If you do that, you can't go wrong. It's helps to be curious," Daniel replied.

"I smile now when I think of myself struggling with depression, though really it was just a year ago. I used to lie on the couch and read my favorite books by inspirational authors. These authors talked about purpose all the time, about everybody having one."

"I was used to life disappointing me and somehow thought that I would, in some way or another, be left out of the loop, kept out of life's inner circle, because I had no real direction," said Lea.

"Seek and you shall find, as the proverb goes," commented Jon.

"So how can one identify one's purpose?" asked Lea meaningfully.

"Ask yourself, what do you enjoy doing that you would do even if you didn't get paid for it? What do other people say you're really good at? What is the one thing you want to experience, or do, or accomplish, before you die, so that on your last day on earth you feel satisfied and have no regrets in that area?" Daniel said.

"We want to coach kids our age in self-defense."

"My greatest hope is to help train women in poor areas to run early childhood development centers."

"I would like to teach impoverished communities to rear goats for milk, bees for honey, or keep chickens for eggs.

"I want to show people how they can be the leaders of their own futures."

"I want to write a book on how people can find their direction in life. But I haven't yet figured out how to do that. In the meantime, I'm willing to devote my time to learning about spirituality and psychology in the hope that I could find myself... to influence nations to win wars before they emerge!"

"Don't worry if you don't have all the answers you seek right now. Keep asking questions. Keep your eyes open for clues. The answers will show up, in perfect time. I promise you." Daniel said.

"How will we recognize our life purpose? What exactly is it?"

"I believe it is simply the driving force during your existence on Earth. Call it a life direction, if you will. Your age is immaterial. You can be 15, 40, 60, or older. It also doesn't matter who you are, where you're from, or what you do. As long as you wish to live a more meaningful and conscious life, knowing your life purpose is important for you."

"Some people just want to live life as it happens and ignore everything else. They just want to chill out and relax until they die."

***

The one-month working holiday at the Beit Nir Kibbutz in Israel had come to an end. The five friends had packed their belongings and stood outside the dining hall. Daniel and Rachel insisted on driving them to the airport.

The teenagers had mixed feelings about leaving the place. So much had happed over the past four weeks. Memories were made. Friendships were formed. But there was one glaring difference.

Their appearances had undergone complete transformations. The black skinny jeans ripped at the knees; tee shirts imprinted with outrageous graphics of skulls or

Hollywood icons, and cropped leather biker jackets had been relegated to the recycle bin. The boys' partially shaved heads showed a certain amount of growth, while the girls' former Harajuku hairstyles in crimson and various other colors were now natural.

Conversation during the trip to the airport was animated and lively. Daniel pointed to the ruins of the ancient city of Mareshah where Zach and Jon were separated from Emma, Lea and Connor. The friends laughed.

"We never did get to see the caves," Zach remarked. Rachel proceeded to tell them that they had missed seeing something truly spectacular.

"Knowing you has given me great hope for the future –for in you are the seeds of change, the potential for a quantum metamorphic and ground-breaking leap for the human species. Your young lives are like a caterpillar becoming a butterfly," Daniel said.

The friends hugged and said their farewells. The airport was unusually quiet. Passengers were called over an intercom to collect their respective boarding passes.

"What we will become we do not now know at our present conscious level, but we can dare to imagine."

"Did the acorn know it would become a mighty oak?"

"In the words of Plato, courage is about knowing what not to fear!"

"But you've got to know when it's time to turn the page."

"Remember, when confronted by the old way of being in

the world or when survival is threatened, to rise above the limitations to become a '(wo)man of knowledge'," Daniel advised.

Chapter V

Spiritual Counterculture

It was one of the coldest days in recorded history; the first day of a new year. The traffic from Heathrow to central London was bumper-to-bumper. Emma looked at the frost-laden tree branches in wonder. It was magical and gruesome at the same time. Her eye caught a lone robin clinging for dear life to an iced branch. She wondered where birds would find food and shelter in this harsh landscape.

A group of revelers staggered along the sidewalk, shouting and laughing. They looked awkward dressed in ankle-length black padded parkas and Cossack boots, their faces pale and gaunt. They were clearly drunk and oblivious that a thief had unceremoniously snatched one of the girls' sling-bag and had sprinted into the stationery traffic. The cab driver had also witnessed the crime, but simply turned his attention to the massive fireworks displays that had erupted, lighting up the night sky.

A cacophony of screams emanated as Big Ben announced the start of the New Year. People embraced.

Swigs from bottles of alcohol were shared among strangers. Their exaggerated smiles looked grotesque, like menacing monkeys about to kill.

The sidewalk was littered with merrymakers lying comatose on the ground, being trodden on by passersby as if they were garbage.

A homeless man peered from behind a pillar, looking horrified as if the street was being invaded by apocalyptic zombies. A toddler stood alone crying. Nobody noticed, or cared. The noise of cars tooting was deafening. Had it been an air raid siren no one would have responded to the warning, or worse, have any place of safety to seek shelter. Emma imagined the carnage if a terror attack were to occur at this precise moment. She never liked crowds.

At last the cab edged forward. Mounted police had been summoned to control the crowd. One rider brought his horse to rest at the side of the cab. Emma raised her head and looked up into the anxious eyes of this majestic animal. Her immediate thought was that it was misplaced among all this chaos and that it belonged in nature far from human cruelty and madness. The animals' eyes flicked from side to side. He was probably scared and looking for a way to escape. His ears were pinned.

Emma wound down the car window and extended her hand to stroke the horse's flank. "I'm sorry for your distress, for humanity's failures," she whispered.

The traffic light turned green and the cab took a sharp right turn away from the throng of people. The contrast in noise level provided relative peace and quiet, but was short-lived. Ambulances with sirens blaring sped past at great speed.

A stray dog got hit by a truck, and lay writhing and yelping in the road. And then deadly quiet. It was both comforting and ominous.

It was a Sunday. For those observing the Sabbath in modern times, it necessitates attending a church service to worship, whilst for many others it is singled out as a day that is different to the rest of the week. Sunday should have a cadence of its own, calm and quiet so that each individual can escape self-imposed anxieties.

Yet, for many Sunday is a day to catch-up on chores and errands, so what often happens is they lose connection with their family, and to God. Christ said that, at the *end* of this age, only God's *direct intervention* would stop man from destroying all human life from this planet. While Orthodox Jews do not celebrate the Sabbath like Christians, their day of worship is Saturday.

Emma wondered what occurrence would propel people to remember God, recognize the significance of family, and show compassion to every living thing.

The rest of the trip to her apartment, which she shared with an aunt, was uneventful. Emma remembered New Year celebrations spent with her mother. They enjoyed dreaming up bizarre resolutions that would be forgotten almost immediately. Her mother had a wild imagination and always set herself eccentric incentives like wanting enough money to buy Buckingham Palace or inventing a time machine so that she could go back in time to take better care of her health.

Emma, on the other hand, would always aspire to simple desires like smiling more, helping others less fortunate and adopting a mentality of work-hard-until-you-succeed.

Following the working-holiday in Israel, she was now even more committed to take on challenges outside her comfort zone in an effort to grow and improve.

Emma wondered what Zach, Lea, Connor and Jon were doing?

Zach was met by his brother at Dallas /Fort Worth International Airport. His heart sank at the sight of the long line of people leaving the security check-out. To kill time the two boys headed for the food court where they treated themselves to pizza. The conversation was very animated. The brothers had a lot in common, both adept at livestock management and off-road motorcycle racing.

Zach's accounts of events that had taken place in Israel had his brother in fits of laughter.

The conversation changed from lighthearted banter to serious deliberation when Zach was informed that three drones were spotted flying too close to airplanes landing at the airport the previous weekend. The drone spotting had prompted suspicions from federal aviation officials, that the unmanned aircraft might pose a threat to commercial planes. Although many of these encounters are not malicious in nature, they call attention to potential security vulnerabilities.

"The FAA must toughen up the rules before a disaster occurs!" he commented.

"Yeah, a drone sucked into a jet engine of a passenger plane will cause untold tragedy," said his brother.

"What happened to your punk get-up? You now look every

bit like a seasoned Texas Drover!"

"Things change. I've built up my friendship with Connor, Lea, Emma and Jon. We think the same about how we can help tackle problems affecting the environment, and life in general."

"Good for you! Never doubt that your small group can do a lot of good. It is precisely the actions of thoughtful, committed people that can make the world a better place."

"It's the only thing that ever has brought about significant change!"

The long check-out line had lessened considerably. The security process was swift. Zach grabbed his tog bag and the boys headed for the parking lot.

"Why did you go away?"

"So that I can come back. So that I can see the place I come from with new eyes."

"And don't forget, the new people you encountered in Israel also see you differently."

"True. Life sets its own challenges to test our courage when we least expect it. Being interrogated for hours on end and kept in a wire cage was not fun."

"Was raking chicken poop the highlight of your holiday?"

"In a bizarre way, washing and sorting hundreds of eggs taught me a lot about life. That labor is a bridge between the individual and society. I found beauty and meaning even in the most menial of tasks, and dignity in a job well done. I'm thinking of starting up a commercial poultry farm, if Dad agrees."

"The hard work surely had its benefits. It sparked in you a willingness to change."

"Life does not look back. A month at the Kibbutz was more than enough time to accept our destiny."

"Fortunately we always have choices to propel our destiny. It's a single-minded decision to get up early each morning, apply yourself to doing something productive like grow your own food, start a poultry business, or simply experiment with tactics to ease widespread problems," Zach's brother said.

"Sometimes it's necessary to become a bit desperate, even forceful, to get ahead. Some problems threatening humanity can no longer be put on the backburner. Young people must be hands-on, creative and tireless in their efforts."

"Many kids our age are easily swayed by promises of a cherished life, made by radical religious groups. They run away from their families to join these groups hoping to find spiritual meaning in their life, and become part of a cohesive ordered community. Modern society has failed to provide them with meaning."

"We're lucky. Our family has a solid religious foundation. But there are kids who don't have any direction.

Those that join militant groups become uber-religious and kill people in the name of their god."

"It is a conscious choice to join these radical groups, and it usually ends in disaster. The new radical ideology of hate and intolerance they think is idyllic eventually raises moral questions, but it is often too late to revert."

"People need to recognize where freedom of speech ends and where hate speech takes over. There's a fine line it seems between radicals, extremists and terrorists."

"Violence, in the name of religion, has become a strategy to boost the terrorists' morale."

Zach observed the view of the countryside as it sped by. It was as if his surroundings were new to him. He suddenly became aware of Texas' extraordinary size. Its population exceeded 25 million people. Zach understood that while the State of Texas was well supplied with raw materials for the production of petrochemical and chemical goods, exploiting these natural resources created negative environmental impacts.

Texas is the largest emitter of carbon in the United States. The massive oil refineries of the Gulf coast and burn-off from oil and gas fields are issues unique to Texas. Besides contaminating the air, airborne emissions leach from the atmosphere into water, soil, crops and livestock, thereby creating secondary issues.

"I worry about the high levels of mercury in our water? Fish and shellfish become inedible. It causes mass kill-offs of fish and animals and an increase in invasive flora."

"Cross-contamination from waste introduces potentially lethal bacteria such as E. coli into water that is eventually consumed by humans."

"The pollution issue is made worse by massive factories and assembly plants located on the Mexican side of the border. Their by-product pollutants are introduced into United States air and the water of the Rio Grande River."

"Companies responsible for the pollution pay high levies, but this does not solve the problem. Ironically, it's cheaper to pollute than to not pollute. In other words, companies are paid to create environmental problems."

The homestead at the end of a long straight road, flanked by a vast expanse of tall Red Oak trees, came into view. Zach remembered when the tree saplings were first planted. It was the year he started junior school. Now, a decade later the forest that had been created presented a visually appealing display of reddish brown foliage that shrouded the thoroughfare in dappled shade. The architecture of the Tuscan farmhouse was designed in a village concept. The style of house was ostentatious, but no different to the rest in this part of Texas. The terraced gardens instilled a sense of tranquility.

Zach saw his parents and younger siblings standing on the patio, waving frantically. It was good to be home. His sense of family had always been strong. They were always there when no one else was, and quite possibly the only people who would ever be there for him, through thick and thin. His thoughts turned to Daniel and Rachel back in Israel, and the four friends he grew to love as family these past four weeks.

Jon arrived at Durban's King Shaka International Airport. The shuttle service had just left, so he sauntered to the taxi rank where he joined a group of airport personnel waiting for a mini-bus taxi.

It was a sweltering hot day in KwaZulu-Natal. The taxi

rank was noisy and disorganized.

South Africans are generally flamboyant; their behavior extroverted. No conversation is private or exclusive. An exchange of opinions, reprimands, questions and laughter is loudly projected for all and sundry to hear. Jon accepted this behavior as part of his culture. It was mostly colorful and entertaining to be privy to people's involvements, and it provided a comfortable sense of familiarity.

The journey to the settlement where he lived took longer than usual. The mini-bus made numerous stops and detours, refueled and waited for a new intake of passengers before eventually resuming the route to central Durban and Inanda.

Patience was a mild precondition compared to mind-numbing tolerance for keeping your sanity.

Jon was amused as he observed two elderly tourists who had got into the taxi at the airport.

Listening to their occasional remarks they were German. They were clearly frightened, especially every time the driver shouted at potential passengers by calling out the destination. Eventually the driver headed for central Durban, a short trip that usually takes under 30 minutes.

"Next stop, Hilton Hotel. Walnut Road!"

The German couple nodded profusely. Their stressed expressions transformed. Jon was undecided whether it was the announcement that the next stop was their intended destination, their relief to have survived the journey in a death trap vehicle, or being freed from listening to two hours of deafening African hip hop music.

The couple glanced at Jon, sensing reciprocated empathy for the situation.

"Auf Wiedersehen!"

"Goodbye."

"Hab ein gutes Leben."

"You have a good life too."

The streets of the rundown settlement were crowded with residents. Inanda Township had become known as one of the most violent places to live. Crimes like hijacking, murder, robbery and domestic violence had become normal occurrences.

A gunshot rang out. A woman screamed and came running to where the crowd had congregated. She was holding an infant in her arms; the child's body was limp.

The Police arrested a young man. The offender did not resist capture. He looked disturbed and stared blankly ahead. The residents watched the tragedy unfold with bland indifference. It was just another day fueled by deprivation, much the same as the day before and the day before that.

No one ventured to commiserate with the mother. Her baby was dead. Her wailing fell on deaf ears. Jon stood rooted to the spot. He did not know how to help this woman. He also could not bring himself to walk by and ignore her plight.

An eerie silence swept over this fragmented place that he now also called home. The change in ambience felt like a breath of fresh air. The sun shone brighter. The unsightly mounds of rotting garbage were a mere figment of the imagination. It was as if the sorrowful mood had been swept away.

Jon looked up and saw his mother standing in the distance, her arms outstretched. He ran to embrace her. She looked thin but healthy and content. His mind raced. Jon felt guilty for having been to Israel and travelling in luxury while his family lived in the worst conditions.

Households had no running water and no electricity. Residents had to walk a fair distance to collect water from a communal tap. The place was unsanitary. Raw sewerage poured from broken pipes. Primitive outside toilet facilities were badly constructed, and unsafe. The roads were impassable due to rubble and garbage being left uncollected.

People were rightfully angry. Their health was being compromised. They had no prospects to escape poverty. Their children were always sick. Protesting had little effect on the local authorities. This community of over 600 000 households were the rejects of a geologically affluent country.

Without negotiation mother and son turned to the distraught woman. They guided her back to her shack. The infant was wrapped in a blanket and placed in a crib. The one-room house was neat and clean. It was sparsely furnished.

The woman confessed that her baby had been sick for days and would not eat. She had planned to take the child to the clinic that day, but he had died a short while ago. The man the police arrested was the child's father. He had been unemployed for the past six years. He had convinced himself he was weak and a worthless father, and attempted to take his own life when he saw his dead son.

Jon vowed that he would apply his knowledge of farming to empower the people living in Inanda. The first project would be to rid the township of garbage and improve sanitation. *"We must all join forces, learn to do things for ourselves, instead of expecting Government to fix our broken lives,"* he said.

The time spent at the Kibbutz had activated Jon's belief that humanity is in need of a new kind of evolutionary leap. *"What must happen to enlighten the hearts and souls of humanity, so that they may recognize their role in the bigger scheme of things?"* he wondered.

Despite his young age, Jon had come to understand that a new kind of intelligence had to be adopted by steering the spiritually deprived. However, most people today have become inert to new ideas; they are dependent on handouts to survive. Many believe they are entitled to lifelong compensation, free housing, free education, and free healthcare.

Distraught people especially cling to false beliefs to validate their disastrous circumstances. Jon was grateful that his parents had instilled in him and his siblings independent thought and the willpower to overcome adversity. He realized that it was going to be an upward battle to dispel entrenched perceptions among his despondent neighbors and fellow residents.

Jon was pleasantly surprised at the homely atmosphere his parents had created in the small house.

The walls were freshly painted. The torn and faded

upholstery on the couches was hidden by brightly colored sheeting. Rows of plastic rain gutters had been mounted against the outside back wall, to grow an assortment of vegetables and herbs.

"We enjoy fresh lettuce and tomato salad every day."

"I hope other residents will catch on to this idea. Food poverty causes malnutrition and often leads to death, especially children younger than five."

"Diseases are very common in people living in poverty. Poor sanitation conditions increase the chance of contracting a disease. Kids here don't attend school. Most people living here go through life illiterate."

"Obtaining a basic education could bring 171 million people worldwide out of poverty."

"A high unemployment rate hinders a country from developing a strong economic system, or progressing in all other aspects."

"South Africa's destitute communities are told by our leaders and the media that their problems are due to inequality, the economic divide that separates the rich and the poor. It has been labeled the prime social ill that must be overcome at all cost, even if it means crippling the country through industry strikes and violent civil unrest."

"This phenomenon is found worldwide. Governments opt to aggressively tax thriving companies, especially small to medium ones, in order to penalize them for being hardworking and enterprising; they forget these businesses also provide much-needed job creation."

"The poor must adopt a different understanding of the implications of inequality. Workers need the intervention of successful businesses to develop skills and earn wages. They are not entitled to their wealth."

"No sane, compassionate person would object to lifting the poor out of poverty and reducing inequality; it would benefit the poor and the rich. Yet, striving to achieve equality is a misnomer. We are too different in our abilities, aspirations and personalities to construct a level playing field. In fact, the world would be a dismal boring place if inequality could ever be eradicated."

"Innovation and creativity would come to an end, which would halt progress, enthusiasm to learn and the pioneering of new ventures, and consequently the gainful employment of ordinary people. However, inequality created through the impoverishment of others—in other words, blatant exploitation—is criminal."

"My time spent at the Kibbutz revealed that humanity needs a revival of secular spiritualism. This would necessitate taking a few steps back to reassess modern traditions that clearly are not working."

"That's an idea. Many seem to have given up on trying to fix social problems that are spinning out of control."

"We need to build new models of coexistence and sustainability, share our unique gifts and reconnect with the wholesomeness of nature and desirable qualities in each other."

"Do you mean reverting back to pre-industrial traditions?"

"In a way, yes. By creating a Spiritual Counterculture that retains digital age literacies applied more socially responsible, more acutely aware of modern day challenges such as terrorism and climate change, solutions to pitfalls might become evident."

"Kids today, the future leaders of the human race, despise spiritual deadness, materialism, and fearfulness. Trauma and turmoil in the world today are two powerful guiding forces steering people toward a Spiritual

Awakening."

"How is your notion of a Spiritual Counterculture different from the Hippie counterculture of the 1960s?

"All I know about the Hippie culture is what I've read in history books!"

"People must be taught to develop a new spiritual outlook, become less materialistic and more compassionate, and more concerned with helping others than fulfilling their own desires and ambitions."

Jon knew he had his work cut out for him. It would not be an easy task but he was excited at the prospect of helping Inanda residents turn their lives around.

Mighty things grow from small beginnings.

He was reminded of a story his grandfather had told him. A landlord instructed his gardener to plant a specific bush. It wasn't a plant with lush foliage and sweet-scented blooms, but a plain nondescript shrub. The gardener was reticent, and of course the landlord asked why he appeared reluctant. The gardener explained that it was a poor choice. *"This stubby shrub is a slow grower and only blooms once every 100 years!"* The landlord was unperturbed. *"Well then, there's no time to lose. Plant it at once!"*

Lea and Connor travelled together, arriving at Australia's Tullamarine International Airport, excited to see familiar surroundings.

The friends had planned to meet up with their respective families to show Connor Mount Dandenong, nestled between the tourist towns of Olinda and Kalorama, and other sites in Melbourne.

The native Australian bush, mountainous environment and surrounding forests were spectacular.

Lunch at the Sky High Restaurant, amidst beautiful formal gardens, was a welcome relief after the long walk.

Connor was drawn to the Denong Arboretum with its 16 hectares of deciduous trees and conifers; it reminded him of the orange grove in Israel. In alternating narrative Connor and Lea gave a concise outpouring of their Kibbutz holiday, which prompted a profound question.

"If you were ruler of the world what laws would you change?" Lea's father asked.

"Actually, I wouldn't bother to change a thing. In putting all things in their proper perspective, it makes sense that immoral control and manipulation of the global social order must intensify and become so overwhelmingly bad before nations unite to eventually say 'Enough!', and awaken to the wisdom of choosing good and rejecting evil by means of their own experience."

"If anything, I would follow the plan Christ outlined from the very beginning, simply explained in scripture. I would spell out more fully the principles of a Spiritual Counterculture … and the gospel so that all might understand His truth and wisdom."

"The most important work we can do in this life is to bring about awareness of human values. There is no denying that our present global society is facing a lot of crises. At the end of the day, it is the quality of human values that will save mankind."

"The test is to achieve unity among living and non-living creatures of the world with the preservation of ethnic and cultural differences. Such unity is the key to driving human values such as truth, kindness, benevolence, peace, love, dignity, respect, and forgiveness."

Connor noticed that his parents were on edge.

It was only when Lea and her parents left the restaurant to head home that he had the opportunity to speak to his parents in private.

He had an unsettling premonition that something bad had happened which they were not telling him.

His mother looked as if she was about to become hysterical. She paced the floor waiting for the elevator to take them to the basement parking garage.

His father was talking non-stop about the weather, the excellent seafood buffet and how healthy Connor looked.

Connor was puzzled at his father's incessant ramblings; something which was totally out of character.

"What on earth is going on?"

"We're flying to Tokyo, tonight!"

"What? Why?"

"We've found Judith. She's been in a hospital in Tokyo for the past three years."

"Daddy hired a detective to go to Tokyo to find out what had happened to her."

"In all this time she's had amnesia. When police found her she couldn't identify herself."

"Apparently she'd sustained a hard blow to the head. There had been a car accident as she left the airport soon after she first arrived in Tokyo."

"Are you sure it's Judith?"

"Yes. Yes."

"The Tokyo Police refer to her as the mystery woman."

"The description they gave us is perfect. White female who stands about five feet, seven inches tall. Her hair and eyes are brown. She weighs about 120 pounds."

"We spoke to her attending physician. She was fortunate to have come out of her coma after two months, with no brain damage, except she had no memory of who she was and what she was doing in Tokyo. She's been a permanent resident in the hospital staff quarters, helping take care of young patients."

"Has she regained her memory?"

"Watching a documentary in English triggered her memories … why I can't imagine. The film was about a young boy who saved a village from deforestation by planting seeds."

"Let's bring her home!"

Chapter VI

Value of Significance

At the dawn of the 21st Century the world has entered into its darkest, most violent period. Racial conflict, terrorism, dictatorships, pillaged economies, and the collapse of state controlled enterprises has made countries worldwide ungovernable.

Escalating environmental exploitation, famine, and accelerated extinction of animal species, human trafficking and crime tighten the noose to hasten the end of life on earth as we know it.

Social experts contend that the 21st Century will continue to bear witness to exponential scientific and technological growth, incomparable to any previous time in human history.

However, the pendulum can swing either way. On the one hand, this growth might exacerbate present-day unruliness, chaos, civil hostilities, famine and disease, whilst on the other hand it could awaken humanity into bringing together a period of humanistic collaboration, spiritual enlightenment and fairmindedness.

Connor, Lea, Zach, Emma and Jon had made a pact that each would seek the value of significance to fulfil a specific objective role in the unfolding future of humanity.

They took their inspiration from the fact that people today, especially young people, are starved for leadership and a meaningful life's purpose.

However, people who have endured hardships and trauma in the past may find themselves emotionally bankrupt if they should face yet another arduous challenge. Some may not have survival mechanisms in place to weather the storm, and willingly allow the unanimous tide to shape the next stages of their life.

But then there are those exceptional individuals who bravely decide to follow a path less travelled to actively seek new fertile ground, and apply lessons learned from life experiences, and draw on the source of absolute knowledge in an attempt to make this world a better place.

In reading *"Go Ahead, Rock the Boat!"* one encounters diverse issues that are of major concern to people today, especially younger generations, revealed through informal conversations. These discussions are the five teenage friends' gateway to validating sentiments, and hence discovering something bigger than themselves.

What started out as a spur-of-the-moment reunion, combined with a 4-week working-holiday in Israel, quickly evolved into a life-changing release from conceit, herd mentality, and opting for easy solutions.

GenZ want to be different to kids younger than themselves and adults, while they readily relate to kids their own age.

In fact, they follow conventional values by what they read, wear, drink, eat, watch, listen to and buy. For advice and guidance they turn to those peers they admire, who are confident, forward thinking and informed. It's human nature after all to try to emulate individuals we admire, to learn by example, through observation and modelling.

Alternatively, whatever your age, it is incumbent upon yourself to ask the burning question, "How can ordinary citizens awaken humanity into bringing together a period of humanistic collaboration, spiritual enlightenment and fairmindedness?"

First, ask yourself whether you ever feel like some form of mass psychosis has descended on a large sector of the population? Look around you, at the facial expressions and body language of people in everyday life. Not just politicians and people in authority, but ordinary citizens, families, your friends and colleagues, even children.

Things that would normally rouse annoyance or at least constructive deliberation are simply accepted as normal or too big a problem for any one person to oppose. It's become too much effort to challenge even the slightest transgression. Does this mean humanity has been successfully duped into submission?

Ask yourself, "Do I object to being fed obvious lies that insult my intelligence, and threaten my survival and human rights?" You know the propaganda is absurd yet the powers that be shower you with legal jargon to show you what will happen if you fail to comply. So you think about it for a moment, and join the ranks of disgruntled people, and do nothing.

Think back to a time before the mass media indoctrinated our minds, before television and radio broadcasts shaped our opinions, before computers, movies and the Internet made us doubt ourselves.

Now alleged experts dictate how we should and should not behave. We tolerate transgressions lest our reaction might hint at denouncing political correctness.

We must conform for our own good, they say. It's not said in a threatening manner but rather veiled as a promise of a brighter, albeit subverted, future. We're duped into believing that the path to a united global populace is to instill traditional values, which seems feasible at first glance, but the aim is not to preserve specific customs and principles relevant to a national culture, but rather instill traditional values that are the same across the board for all of humanity. One identity. One uniform global society.

Are events that impact humanity as a whole therefore part of some master plan?

Conspiracy theorists, along with a few truly enlightened and investigative individuals, believe that the *shadow world government* orchestrates events to control human population numbers through reproductive awareness, alarmism or intentionally reducing the bulk of the world population through genocides, pandemics, environmental disasters, and launching war against vulnerable and ill-prepared nations.

Most countries are playing into the hands of these unscrupulous oppressors by following an agenda that appears logical and industrious on the surface. Combating poverty; adopting alternative consumption patterns; promoting health; strengthening the roles of indigenous peoples, women and youth; and systematically evacuating people from rural areas to allegedly seek a more prosperous life in urban areas.

Crowded urbanization is a conscious move to create untenable development, widening inequalities in income, racial conflict and continued deterioration of society and the environment. Social critics accuse governments and corporations of instilling a culture of fear in people to achieve political and economic goals. Lawlessness, unemployment, homelessness, economic decline, threat of infectious disease, and food poverty are but a few negative entities that hold people captive in the grip of fear.

Governments therefore keep the masses ignorant—offering platitudes to quell social, emotional, or cognitive unease—as a way to stay in power.

These deceptive governments discourage exceptionalism and individualism through diffusion that there are no perfect heroes and no perfect victims. They tug away at the fragments left for humanity to reclaim their God-given right for spiritual enlightenment and living a purposeful and significant life.

Adversity and failure makes their citizens have second thoughts about their potential. All this leads to no one having power, and the only thing left is not the individual, just the community.

Most people adhere to a herd mentality, by accepting any

farcical solution to anything without question. They don't consider alternative outcomes. Instead they follow a prescribed routine that is deemed acceptable and safe, until repercussions prove otherwise.

People have become so habituated that the demise of millions from starvation and disease draws no more than a sigh of boredom or a jibe at poor people's incompetence to be self-sufficient.

Yet a thousand brutish horrors wipe out people who are privileged, by way of substance abuse, chronic disease, and eating disorders at a rate not seen since the Dark Ages.

Our modern creative culture is at best derivative. Our architecture is uninspiring. Our clothes are mediocre. New discoveries that have the potential to cure cancer and other diseases, replace fossil fuels and produce abundant food inexpensively, are deliberately held under wraps.

While periods in history mirror similar kinds of indifference, our time is the first to have the technology and resources to educate, employ, feed and house every person on earth. Yet, feasible ideas and proven technologies that can meet these expectations are not developed because it is more economically viable to keep the wheels of consumerism grinding away.

Conformity is a convenient condition to manipulate people as a whole. Habitual behavior keeps them from questioning decisions made on their behalf. However, if we allow this psychosis to continue, the *shadow world government* will have won the battle. If we do not awaken from our mesmerized slumber we are nothing more than Zombie-like people roaming the earth, unaware of our fate.

Humanity is coming apart at the seams; people are rendered incapable of thinking for themselves. We've become complacent.

It's easier to follow the crowd than it is to pursue a self-sufficient existence. We've become spoiled through convenience, so we simply adapt to working harder, paying more, slowly eroding our true purpose in life.

Ask yourself, *"How would I recognize if I'm living in a country that is pulling the wool over my eyes?"* When your President starts acting like a dictator and his underlings don't oppose the rampant corruption. When poverty is out of control; that the poorest of the poor go without bread to buy a lotto ticket instead—in the hope of winning the jackpot.

When a potential labor force is deliberately demotivated to develop job skills by keeping them dependent on welfare instead. When rape and murder is accepted as a common crime, justified as a reaction to inequality, poverty and poor education. When exploitation of targeted groups are kept out of the news, allegedly to avoid public panic.

When farm murders are rampant, and nothing is done to safeguard the people who grow the food the rest of the nation needs to survive. When wild animals are poached for financial gain. When governments of poor nations are overthrown to steal their natural resources, such as oil and precious metals.

Similarly, oil extraction is known to cause deforestation and environmental devastation of lands across the globe, resulting in the release of toxic by-products into local rivers. Spills from burst pipelines pollute the surrounding lands and waterways, wreaking havoc on aquatic ecosystems.

There is no respect for the environment, and little respect for one another.

Pick up any newspaper or view the news on television to remind yourself of the reasons that make this world an insane place to live and rear children.

Individuals who belong in mental institutions walk among us. They are often dangerous and vulnerable to abuse and exploitation, yet have no support system to provide them with a safe haven and protect the general public from them; and us from them. Instead they are left to their own devices. It is precisely this form of human behavior that will influence young people toward making this world a better place.

Albeit, young people today are exposed to diverse forms of communication each day. While much of serious news is perhaps beyond their comprehension to untangle and debate with knowledge and maturity, kids are more aware than they are given credit for.

Consequently, young people listen and learn from people they admire and trust, which helps them enhance their interpretation of a certain issue and develop perceptions based on rational thought and objective opinions.

Similarly, GenZ think of celebrities, the rich and famous, as highly regarded role models to compensate for absent parental guidance. These kids build an emotional attachment to public figures, often to the extent that their adoration is labeled abnormal.

Generation Z has been exposed to the acquisition of knowledge since birth, and are acutely aware of the importance of staying abreast of current affairs, in particular social change that might impact their progress. They read books, magazines and newspapers, listen to the radio, watch television, and enjoy thought-provoking films based on a portrayal of how they view and propose to shape human existence.

They also browse the Internet to expand their knowledge, and profit from validation by reading interviews with famous people.

Connor, Lea, Zach, Emma and Jon are prime examples of how teens are able to focus their ideas on finding solutions to global problems. Bear in mind that the vast majority of teens today spend most of their day in school, among like-minded peers.

Accordingly, opinions can spread quickly. Scholars from different schools interact through sports and community-based activities. They also network via cellular phone, online forums, chat rooms, and bulletin boards, as well as through extra-mural activities. They have taken the bait that Knowledge is Power.

The five teenagers were stirred by an inner calling to embrace oncoming adulthood with constructive influence to fight the good fight. The jobs they were assigned during their stay at the Kibbutz compelled them to step out of their comfort zone. But it's not until they come face-to-face with unnerving situations that their mindsets take on a new understanding of the connectivity between the belief of ideological conviction and human existence.

Realizing the connection triggered a leap into an altered state of awareness. In their own unique way they had conquered fear and learned to question everything. While the veracity of humanity's need for a spiritual awakening truly hit home, the idea of how to go about building new models of coexistence and sustainability by reverting back - to a degree - to pre-industrial traditions was puzzling.

The difficulty of their challenge was emphasized by the logical assumption that modern progress and digital age literacies had to be retained, albeit applied more socially responsibly. Constructive progress that has brought the human race thus far can't simply be wiped out or rejected.

This concept places a direct responsibility at the feet of every person living today. Planning the way forward is heavily reliant on reassessing destructive habits and putting an emergency plan into action. The collective effect of bringing adverse principles to a close will eventually topple the control of greedy world leaders and corrupt organizations that steer global business and finance, politics, war and peace, and religious ideologies.

Asking questions and assessing feedback is the key. By evaluating the conversations within the context of the *"Go*

Ahead, Rock the Boat!" storyline you not only establish a corresponding bond through the cultural diversity personified by the characters Connor, Jon, Emma, Lea and Zach, you also uphold your individuality with the intention of actualizing your life's purpose.

On a personal level it is incumbent upon every citizen on earth to embrace, teach, and practice values that bring human existence into balance by adapting philosophies and traditions and rediscovering true religion in a world that has become atheistic, as a way of resolving problems.

We must begin to redirect indoctrinated beliefs within our own family units.

However, not all human beings are endowed with reason and conscience.

To establish such values and the ethical standards that protect all human beings for the 21st century we must be prepared to learn from the past, evaluate the present, and project the highest and best that we know into our aspirations for the future.

We must examine our values on the basis of international, national, and personal commitments.

In theory, the idea of building new models of coexistence and sustainability by reverting back to pre-industrial traditions is simply to determine where human advancement went astray.

The world prior to the Industrial Revolution was a very different place to the one that exists today. Food was produced locally; not the genetically modified crops that are produced *en masse* today, to feed close on 9-billion mouths, driven by an increasing demand for protein-rich produce.

Clothing was made locally; not to the extent that the global manufacture of textiles have grown today, to mass-produce garments mostly bypassing the application of clean technologies and using eco-friendly raw materials.

It is also an industry that engages in illegal child labor, and exposes workers to poor working conditions and low wages.

What was manufactured was done making use of natural elements, such as windmills. There were no cars, airplanes, trains or tarmac roads. Education was poor even then. Politics was based mainly upon land ownership.

Communities were reliant upon each other; people worked in villages and small towns, and on the land; not the widespread division we know today that alienates the worker from their humanity. Our modern capitalist society has reduced the labor of the worker to an article of trade rather than as a constructive socio-economic activity for personal survival and the betterment of society.

The world population was also significantly smaller compared to an estimated eight billion people within less than a decade; this number will likely reach around nine billion by 2037. Since the 250 years from the beginning of the Industrial Revolution to today, the world human population has increased by six billion people.

We have learned from the past and the present what tragedies can develop when the population exceeds the ability of a nation to provide employment, education, food, housing, healthcare, and social development for all its citizens. Human overpopulation silently intensifies harsh conditions like environmental pollution, mass species extinction, lower life expectancy among poorer nations, increased emergence of new epidemics and pandemics, increased crime rate, intensive farming practices and over-fishing, deforestation, over-consumption of fresh water and fossil fuels, which in turn can and do affect changes in climate locally and possibly even globally.

Although the Industrial Revolution brought with it many advances to our modern society, it also brought with it many setbacks for humanity and the natural environment.

Just like Connor, Lea, Zach, Emma and Jon are representative of how each individual has the capability to make a difference in creating a new and better future, it is hoped that this narrative has also inspired you, the reader, to seek extended answers to questions like: *"Where am I going? How can I improve my circumstances? How can I inspire others to fully embrace their humanity?"*

Conversely, it is short-sighted to assume that solutions to big problems are set in stone; many questions that are relevant today might warrant systematic re-evaluation in the future, depending on the context.

The challenge lies in analyzing each new answer to reveal the starting point to further investigation to ask much bigger questions. Hence, Absolute Knowledge is based on the continual process of asking more reflective questions.

Religion, politics, and even philosophy, provides convenient well-rehearsed gross answers to pertinent questions, based on the prevailing collective social conviction.

Most people accept 'educated' explanations without question; yet, a desire to challenge dubious revelations always surfaces at the point of conflict, when answers appease rather than incite opposition and determination to move forward.

Most people resist change, claiming that radical transformation is for the most part problematic in one way or another. Yet, it is stagnation and refusal to change that fuels failure.

Revolutions, of the beneficial and constructive kind, are made by asking radically new questions. This kind of wisdom is what will take humanity beyond the horizon.

Who or what is behind the widespread mayhem putting down roots worldwide?

The future of the world, more so its impending downfall, hinges on the impulses and subjective agendas of powerful corrupt world leaders and select influential groups that impact global business and finance, politics, war and peace, religious ideologies, and control of the world's resources and its money.

Their hankering for wealth and power expresses little or no concern for human wellbeing.

These global Capitalist elite surreptitiously create a self-styled, albeit disturbing, reality to supplant individual nation-state sovereignty with an all-powerful global government, corporate controlled, and checkmated by militarized enforcement.

By the same token, a new approach and return to Communism is determined to enforce their grand design to eventually form a One World Government with a single, global marketplace, policed by a one world army, and financially regulated by one central World Bank using one global currency.

Other intended outcomes—some already in motion—include centralized control of world public opinion, manufactured crises and inciting unnecessary wars, control of all foreign and domestic policies, imposing a universal legal system; and a global welfare state where compliant citizens will be rewarded and non-conformists will be targeted for extermination.

Ironically, war has been recognized by military leaders, scientists, philosophers, religious leaders and others as an obsolete way of settling problems—typifying a lose-lose rather than a win-win outcome.

What makes people inclined to obey mass persuasion?

What most people perceive as self-determination and honest public opinion is, in reality, carefully crafted and scripted media propaganda.

Public opinion is swayed and molded by what people are told to believe, and how to respond.

Moral and social behavior in our modern age reflects this, driven by the incredible speed with which things change.

People today are in a perpetual state of ineptitude.

Consider that yesterday's skills repertoire will be outdated tomorrow, which means people must constantly enhance their knowledge and skills to adapt to new expectations. Not everybody can cope with a commitment to lifelong adaptation to change.

People exposed to cycles of accelerated change often develop physical and mental illness, and dependency on external means for survival. They risk becoming victim to exploitation when their individuality is diminished, which means they can be easily controlled and formed into what anyone wants them to be.

Are global populations being coerced on a mass scale to adopt a uniform mindset?

The effect on society as a whole spans a gambit of adverse emotions from violent behavior to helplessness and despair.

A common modern day neurosis is anxiety fueled by irrational fears, often brought on and magnified by media reportage. People are influenced by what they see on television or read in the print media.

Exposure to a daily diet of targeted information has been instrumental in inciting violent behavior, or apathy for that matter. Television reportage distorts reality from fantasy, which effectively clouds people's true judgment.

People fail to recognize dire warnings about humanity's imminent demise by being accepting of disasters and emotionally unresponsive.

The general populace today is distressed and fearful. Many

are destitute and illiterate. They have stopped questioning.

How are people affected by foreign refugees infiltrating their countries of origin?

Developed countries are being invaded by hordes of foreign refugees, among them terrorists intent on replacing that country's culture with their own radical ideologies. In the long run ethnic populations, native to certain countries, are stripped of everything and experience dreadful oppression, resulting in chaos and decline.

Cold-blooded terror attacks and murders occur with such regularity that global populations perceive them as normal, albeit dreadful, assaults. National economies are plundered. Nations are divided, resulting in dissension. In the end, organized civil revolt erupts as xenophobia between nationals and foreign invaders to oppose a repressive government, one that confines people's human rights, is racially biased, takes liberties for self-gratification while the poorest of the poor remain marginalized, and hugely compensates an elitist echelon of corrupt politicians and industry moguls to the detriment of the country and its natural populace.

Is transformation at all possible, to prevent total annihilation of the human race?

First, recognize the enemy for what it is and actively seek to change it in a firm yet empathetic and balanced way.

Even long-established beliefs are not immune from the effects of a global reawakening.

A realistic display of positive consequences through a

return to a natural balanced state could reverse the threat of total annihilation overnight.

Also, we must question the validity of the propaganda we are being fed through the media and civic education. Bear in mind that events of civic interest are engineered and transmitted to perpetuate fear and apathy. Key to this motive is to divert our attention from free thought, and the fact that the planet is being destroyed, citizens are dying of starvation, disease and despair.

Make it your mission to look at the world through new eyes.

Dissect the long term plot to control and destroy humanity:

Reveal the strategies that promote conflict with disobliging countries that are kept secret; the clandestine treaties with alleged enemy governments; the dumping of toxic waste in poor countries; and prohibiting the supply of essential goods to countries dependent on imports.

Screening social ills on a large scale will enable you to identify patterns and link events that the general public is often only privy to as modified interpretations.

Once you can piece together the real agendas behind the smoke screens, your Absolute Knowledge will guide you to educate others to separate fact from fantasy, and reverse negativity and manipulation to develop an energy flow toward embarking on a Hero's Journey.

How will the coming Transformation affect humanity?

The coming Transformation to a unified multi-dimensional

Christ-like consciousness will affect everyone, even powerful corrupt world leaders and global Capitalist or Communist elite.

We can only be controlled or intimidated if we allow ourselves to be so. People's cultures, ethnic groups, religions and economic backgrounds all contribute to shaping a complex set of beliefs, values, and behaviors.

Sometimes we are marginalized because of our cultural influences, which may create obstacles in recognizing and responding to certain circumstances within a diverse society.

Is it possible for humanity today to push a reset button to change the implications of unsustainable growth and dependence on limited resources to revert back to some aspects of a time before the Industrial Revolution and embark on the next revolution, the Era of Sustainability?

The industrialization processes worldwide continue to serve all basic human needs, including food production, medicine, housing and clothing. The most prolific impact on the modern world has been the growth of the human population, which is indelibly tied together with increased consumption of natural and man-made resources, energy, and land for growing food and for living, housing, as well as the exponential increase of waste by-products.

Similarly, excessive consumption demands have a tremendous impact on the environment and ultimately on the health of all living things. Fossil fuels that keep the wheels of industry turning have forever changed the way people live and utilize energy; it has become so firmly interwoven into human progress and economy, that transforming dependence would grind industry to a halt and severely inconvenience the way we live our lives. Yet the ramifications of progress are indelibly connected to how humanity will usher in a new era of sustainability.

Why do older people doubt the potential of young people to make an impact on identifying solutions to eradicate harmful issues that are merging to hasten the destruction of life on earth as we know it?

Ours is a decaying age. Throughout history it has been documented that young people fail to respect their parents. They are rude, entitled and impatient. They are undisciplined, lazy and have no self-control.

Plato, in the fourth century BC, remarked: "What is happening to our young people? They disrespect their elders, they disobey their parents. They ignore the law. They riot in the streets, inflamed with wild notions. Their morals are decaying. What is to become of them?"

Disparaging portrayals are today worse than ever. Our risk-averse culture obliges parents to raise and educate children in 'captivity'. Children have not changed; they still flourish in an unconfined environment, free to discover the wonders of life, but times have changed.

As parents we are riddled with anxieties. We are continually hyper-vigilant. We imbed fear in our children with stories and images of violent and aggressive crimes, of a ruthless world that offers no guarantees of a significant and valued existence. The downside is that kids become frustrated, held back by threats of what might happen.

They are robbed of freedom of expression. They don't form valuable opinions. It is therefore no surprise that children as young as four rebel against inhibited control. Kids adopt aggressive and antisocial behavioral traits. The outcome of this narrow 'protective' upbringing cultivates a belief in young people that they are incapable of independent thought; that they are failures. They are made to feel insignificant and incredibly vulnerable so they become depressed, and aggressive.

How you can contribute to healing the world!

Never doubt than you can make a praiseworthy contribution to help heal the world. While it might sound too easy to be true, it is clear just how troubled our world is. Why? Because of us, the human race. So, it's our responsibility to fix things! Even if you don't add to the devastation directly, you and I are inseparable from those who do.

Hoping to reverse the calamities is as daunting as it sounds. We all need to re-evaluate our habits and beliefs, which may be easier said than done. Reducing meat and fish from our diet is not enough to stop livestock from being slaughtered, often through inhumane practices, or our oceans from being overfished to meet the growing demand of humans' dietary and commercial requirements.

Utilizing solar energy and getting off the grid might be a step in the right direction, but it is still not enough to reverse climate change. Nor is adopting a self-sufficient lifestyle of voluntary simplicity on its own enough, however well-intentioned it may be.

To heal the world we have to change our ways significantly and alter practices that we take for granted, but also go out of our way to edify others in order to create a chain reaction to bring about a positive change worldwide.

The objective is to raise human consciousness by way of endorsing awareness of *sustainability and downshifting* principles so that individuals may rise above the constraints of greed, materialism, fear, violent behavior, hatred, jealousy, and desire for vengeance. To further this goal it is necessary to question everything; acquire absolute knowledge of the relevant principles in question.

Be assertive when taking action. Don't be afraid to rock the boat to obtain answers and solutions. And be prepared to handle profound consequences when you do. Some concerns that irritate and frustrate people include everyday complications as well as complex problems.

Why are our incomes declining? Why is the cost of living skyrocketing? Why are the ranks of the poor swelling? Why are so many people still illiterate in this day and age? Why are many people accepting of discrimination? Why aren't people rebelling against a system that violates their basic human rights? Why is economic gain corrupting our civilization?

How is it possible that a People's Revolution or at least a major wave of reform is not actively being pursued? Why are people retarded in their reaction to rectify injustices? The answers to these questions are simple. The working class is held in abeyance by fear of being further economized; they don't dare rock the boat by lamenting the injustice of corruption.

The unemployed masses have no voice; they are the faceless untouchables of society, deposited out of sight on the periphery of functional society. Working people today delude themselves if they believe they have job security, even if they have a contract to this effect. Employees turn a blind eye to irregularities in the workplace that might get them fired. They know they are expendable.

Young people are notoriously associated with exercising freedom of speech and demonstrating active rebellion to draw attention to social change, but even their voices have been silenced. They are cautioned not to rock the boat, and protect their reputations if they want to be considered for employment in the highly competitive job market as new graduates.

And finally, the general public has become ultra-cynical about government that many no longer believe change is possible. People no longer trust leaders' decisions. Many don't bother to keep track of outcomes that impact their lives. Their contention is that rulings proceed unopposed anyway.

Because most citizens are in a state of perpetual dejection, it is hard to get them energized to jumpstart their bodies and brains to join the good fight and rid the world of the social ills.

Will it take an onslaught of conspiracy realism to bring about a mind shift that will jolt humanity into bringing about radical, meaningful and beneficial social change to heal the earth?

Author's Closing Note

In writing this book my initial intention was to develop a disjointed set of occurrences that would enthrall the reader to easily relate to life's most basic challenges, and in so doing navigate a life of meaning.

But as the story unfolded the distinctive characterizations of the five teenage friends helped develop diverse scenarios that would hopefully stimulate the readers' expansive vision of a personal challenge that they might need to tackle.

Yet for anyone with competence and courage, the risk of venturing into the unknown where the rules and limits are not known, lies in showing willingness.

While grappling with questions pertaining to global events seemingly beyond our control may be construed as a contentious topic, the idea that *sustainability and* downshifting is less perilous than *revolution*, and is more a metamorphic ideal that it is the voice of reason.

But the longer we wait the more likely the fall of the human race will coincide with an *onslaught of cataclysmic proportions*. The world is crying out for genuine Messianic leadership, which would encompass moral and righteous qualities.

It is my sincere wish that *Go Ahead, Rock the Boat!* has inspired you sufficiently to look at the world with new eyes, to embrace new opportunities to grow as a person of significance, and to garner the courage to rebel against circumstances that call for righteous change.

The Hero persona that strives to bring about a Spiritual

Counterculture is the foundation to set the stage for forward-thinking humanitarian leadership.

Michael HH Warren

July 2016

Acknowledgments

To my Lord and Savior who has blessed me with a mind and heart that seeks to share with all who would care to listen and learn.

With heartfelt love and appreciation to Alison, my wife and best friend, and to our children Kelly and Caden, who give me the time and space to research and write.

Finally, I would like to express my sincere thanks to Theresa Lütge-Smith of the South African Writer's Network, for her invaluable contribution to the production of this book; for her assistance in the initial development of the book's framework and for her substantial research.